MW01172721

WALK AS CHILDREN OF THE LIGHT

A Transformational Devotion For Life!

Jay W. Spillers

Executive Writers, LLC.

Copyright © 2022 Jay W. Spillers

All rights reserved

The characters and events portrayed in this book are fictitious. Any similarity to real persons, living or dead, is coincidental and not intended by the author.

No part of this book may be reproduced, or stored in a retrieval system, or transmitted in any form or by any means, electronic, mechanical, photocopying, recording, or otherwise, without express written permission of the publisher.

ISBN: 9798843309657

Cover design by: Art Painter
Library of Congress Control Number: 2018675309
Printed in the United States of America

DEDICATION

*To my loving wife Linda and our son Timothy and to my
parents Harold and Linda who have crossed over to the Light.*

CONTENTS

PREFACE

This book was born out of a dream that I had one night on February 18th, 2021. I prayed before going to bed that night that I would have heavenly lucid dreams, as I've prayed many nights before. Tonight I would dream about "Walking as Children of the Light" here on earth. As the verse in Ephesians 5:8 says, "For you were once darkness, but now you are light in the Lord. Walk as children of light" The dream was narrated to me. In the dream, I saw people playing like children, dancing, and some were just calmly enjoying each other's company. The scene was one of celebration and joy. People seem to be experiencing total bliss. I could see open fields with beautiful green grass growing everywhere. I saw many flowers growing in the field. There were many trees all around. The people were mostly in a central clearing within the trees.

One thing I remember clearly was that the light was shining all around us. The people themselves were also radiating light from within their being.

No one ruled over anyone else in any context. We all guided each other and shared power. There were no titles or hierarchies within this place. Truly, we all lived as brothers and sisters with all equality. All conflicts are solved with unconditional love. There was a total love that came from that place, like nothing I had ever experienced on earth. There was perfect peace in this place and a sense of tranquility. The peace was both an outer peace among people but also a sense of inner peace. The external peace was made possible because of the peace within that everyone was experiencing.

There was a feeling of kindness and compassion that I could feel in the people. There seemed to be no problems going on. Any issue that one can think of in this world was dealt with in love and kindness. This beautiful dream describes heaven on earth. Many may see such a world in the "new earth" to come, or the millennial reign of Christ. The point though was simply not to wait for a perfect time to come, but to help establish a more perfect time right now or try to get it as close as possible as we can in love. (This book is not about eschatology but a quality of living and being for the believer that applies regardless of where we are in God's eschatological time frame) We may not see the full reality of this dream until the new earth, but let us be about the Lord's work seeking to make the world a more loving, kind, and peaceful place where we can. I have often meditated on such things, both before the dream and after. The dream helped to take my heart to deeper levels of my walk in His Light. The verse and dream are much in line with those that have died and went to heaven and then come back to tell us what heaven and God's love are like.

The goal of this book is to open the reality of the dream more fully to you in your own personal life. I also meant it to help you truly grow and walk in the Light and help to transform this world and the world around you into a better place. We all know what world we want to live in, but see a world that falls horribly short of that. It's now time to let our light shine before men and women in a way we all haven't lived up to. The book focuses on illuminating how you can grow in the Light from the scriptures themselves.

I have an excellent new Meditation Course that you can take online at: https://www.udemy.com/course/meditation-basics/?referralCode=BBE42B5D004098552476

You may follow further spiritual discussions with Jay on Facebook at: https://www.facebook.com/Spiritual-Discussion-Page-106913824248676/?modal=admin_todo_tour .

You may also join Jay's NDE Facebook group at: https://www.facebook.com/groups/2588947844768967 You may follow

Jay's podcast "Inspire Me with Jay" at: https://www.podpage.com/inspire-me-with-jay/ You may watch Jay's Youtube Channel at: https://www.youtube.com/user/Spillers72

Walk As Childen of the Light Facebook Group: https://www.facebook.com/groups/427237486089089

INTRODUCTION

When we speak of walking as children of the Light, there are so many questions that come to mind. How do you walk in the Light? What does it mean to walk in the Light? What does walking in the Light look like? What will change in me when I start to walk in the Light? Will the change be immediate or will it be something gradual over time? What will it mean for others around me as I begin to more fully walk in the Light? These questions will be answered throughout this book in many forms, both directly and indirectly.

The qualities of walking in the Light are many and varied. Some of the essential qualities are summed up in the Fruits of the Holy Spirit which are love, joy, peace, patience, kindness, goodness, faithfulness, gentleness, and self-control. (See Galatians 5:22, 23) There're others such as compassion and forgiveness, but the Fruits can give you a good starting point for understanding what walking in this Light is all about. When you start the journey of consciously walking as a child of the Light, everything will change, in mind, heart, words, and actions. Will others notice the changes in me? In many cases, they will notice some changes. In some cases, they may not notice if the changes are gradual, or they're distracted in their own lives. You may notice differences in your relationship with others, you seem calmer around them. There seems to be more peace in the relationship and less conflict. When conflicts arise, they seem to diffuse more quickly because of the way you will react to the situation. You will let go of anger faster and just move on. You will not stew about it like you used to.

How does the change happen in me? Many churches and Christians have gotten caught up in performance-based living. They strive within themselves to live as they should. What some call trying to live the spiritual life out of the "flesh". Some call this a works theology either to gain favor with God or to gain salvation itself. Legalism can quickly set in and you end up not focusing on the inward qualities of love and kindness at all but on external behaviors such as not drinking, smoking, watching certain types of movies, etc. This is one extreme that a believer can fall into and to some extent, I have myself, not for salvation, but to "please" God.

There is another extreme of what I call hyper-grace, it's an all of God's school of thinking. You basically sit back and do nothing, and God is going to one day just completely change you. You take no action at all, just wait on God to move. I've also fallen into this extreme at different times in my Christian walk. I got to the point of thinking, "OK, what do I do? Nothing? Just sit here". This can feel good for a while, but deep down we know this attitude doesn't ring true either.

So what is the balance between these two extremes? I think the balance is to see ourselves as helping to plant the seeds of change in us. We seek to plant qualities that are primarily internal in nature that will reap both internal and external changes in us. God is the one that takes the seed and germinates it from there and makes it grow in us. He needs a receptive heart and mind to work through and will not just override our will. He will not just magically change us. God is the one that gives the harvest though, without question, but it's our job to cooperate with Him.

I have broken this down into three areas of transformation that this book focuses on, not in a strict order. First, we have the transformation of the heart which includes prayer, meditation, inspiration, and the word. Second is the transformation of the mindset which includes making love central to everything, letting go of judgments, and knowing who you are in Christ, and what your position is in Him. You need to be grateful and affirm your gratitude and who you are. There are some actions in the transformation which include living out kindness and allowing for no distractions in your walk. Obviously, the areas of transformation blend and work together. As your heart changes, so does your mindset. As your mindset changes, it affects your heart. Both will result in different actions, as you take action it changes your heart and mind.

Each chapter besides having in-depth teaching on each area will have a key verse to reflect on that is stated at the beginning. The chapters will also end with an application section, which will help you to apply what you've learned in each chapter. This book is a transformational devotional that you will hopefully come back to again and again and not just read once. I recommend keeping a journal to record how your applications go and what is going on in your life to grow in His Light. Now, let's begin the journey of a lifetime that will change everything!

1. BE IN THE LIGHT

"But if we walk in the light as He is in the light, we have fellowship with one another, and the blood of Jesus Christ His Son cleanses us from all sin." (I John 1:7)

To walk as a child of the Light, you must first be in the Light. This may seem obvious, but it's a foundational truth to recognize. Many who have been believers for several years may see much of this chapter as things they already know well. This chapter will cover some quite simple truths, yet they are the most profound ones that need to be addressed.

Don't skip this chapter or just skim over it, try to read it deeply. Though many of the truths will be familiar to you, it's good to hear them again and take time to reflect on them and to pray that they would be understood and a reality in your life. You may be in the Light right now, but seek to go even deeper in his Light, which is the purpose of this book. You may discover old truths, but they take on a new freshness to you.

I may say something that is a familiar truth to you, but it resonates in a way that hasn't in the past. Something may click with you that never has before or not in such a profound way. You may also gain new insights into a truth you already believed that will take your spirit to new heights in your faith. You may also gain your own insights that I don't specifically touch on in this chapter or book as you begin to reflect on these truths and pray that God makes them a greater reality in your life.

BORN OF HIS SPIRIT

The most elemental truth that one needs to have to start

walking in the Light is to know that you must be born of His Spirit. As John 3:3 says "Jesus answered and said to him, "Most assuredly, I say to you, unless one is born [a]again, he cannot see the kingdom of God." Why is being born again or born of his Spirit so important? The passage tells you plainly that you cannot "see the Kingdom of God without" it. What does the kingdom of God mean? Yes, it's heaven. An important aspect of being born again is so that you can go to heaven when you die, no doubt. Is there more to the kingdom of God, though?

The kingdom of God

The scriptures also talk about the kingdom of God being within you. (Luke 17:20, 21) The kingdom of God is a state of being within you, not just a place you go to at the end of life but a place actually within your being itself. Heaven is literally within your heart. Maybe this is why people often speak of "asking Jesus into your heart". They may be hitting on a truth more profound than they even realize! Paul spoke of the kingdom in terms of quality of living as it says in Romans 14:17 "for the kingdom of God is not eating and drinking, but righteousness and peace and joy in the Holy Spirit." Notice he mentions righteousness, peace, and joy. These are just three qualities of the kingdom and not an exhaustive list by any means. When Jesus and his disciples would preach the message of the kingdom, it most assuredly was broader than just going to heaven when you die. Jesus spent so much of his ministry teaching people how they should live now. We see this in the Sermon on the Mount and on his teachings regarding love. We also see it in how we should treat our neighbors. The kingdom is both about life now and life in the world to come.

A New Creation

Closely connected to being born again is when Paul taught on becoming a new creation in II Corinthians 5:17. Everything will become new in your life and the old will pass away. This newness is something that is ongoing and continues from the moment of the new birth. It doesn't stop at the birth but continues to grow in you day by day.

How are you born of his Spirit? The Spirit comes in and begins to work in you in a moment. When you are born again, you are immersed in His love. This is the greatest quality of being born of his Spirit is to take on this life-changing love within you. As we will see, love is central to scripture and the Christian life. Seek this heart of love with all your being, pray for it daily. Meditate on this love and allow it to fully manifest itself within you.

Immersed In His Spirit

When you are born again, you are also immersed in His Light. You come into the Light and can then begin to walk in this Light. What does light do? It dispels the darkness and helps you to see what is before you. It makes everything transparent to you. A huge component of the Light is that you begin to walk in truth. You see things as they truly are within you and things around you. The blinders are now off. To fully transcend in the Light, you must seek to walk further into the Light in your walk with Him. The Light starts at your spiritual birth, but it grows brighter as you continue with Him. Think of the Light as a light at the end of a great tunnel. It may start as a tiny speck of light, but as you walk closer and closer toward the light, it becomes larger and brighter to you. Your journey once you are born of the Spirit and see the pinprick of light is to keep moving closer and closer to it. Jesus will take your hand and help guide you along the way, as will his Spirit.

A third aspect of being born of the Spirit is to be immersed in His peace. Jesus said, "Peace I leave with you, My peace I give to you; not as the world gives, do I give to you." (John 14:27) This is a peace that passes all understanding. (Philippians 4:7). Like love and light, this will be something that starts at your new birth but will continue to grow as you walk with Him. The peace is already there from the beginning, but it's a matter of walking in it and fully manifesting it over time. This peace will unfold to you as you seek Him. Think of it as a beautiful flower. It may start as a bud but eventually will bloom and open up. Allow this peace to fully bloom within your heart and mind!

A fourth aspect of being born of His Spirit is to be immersed in His joy. As I Peter 1:8 says, "Though you have not seen him, you love him; and even though you do not see him now, you believe in him and are filled with an inexpressible and glorious joy". (NIV) Part of being born again is to have unspeakable joy. This doesn't mean you feel happy or joyous at every moment of your life, I wish that were the case, but as you take time with Him and contemplate on Him your joy will grow. The key is to spend time and reflect on Him. These are the times the joy will be intensified in you the most. The more you meditate on Him and his goodness, the more joy you will experience. All the joy is within you at birth, but seek to walk in it.

Feelings and Faith

How important are feelings when it comes to our new life in Christ? We often hear "we live by faith not by feelings". This is a correct statement, you can't always rely on feelings to be there and ultimately we must press ahead in faith. I think we sometimes use such statements, however, to dismiss the importance that feelings can have. Think of all the things you know you should be doing in your faith, such as praying, reading scripture, or helping others. How motivated are you to do those things when you just don't feel like doing it? When you don't feel the love, joy, or peace within you? Yes, you should do those things regardless of how you feel, but it's much easier to do them when you feel good. If Christ promised you joy and peace, which to a great extent involves feelings, then our emotions must be of importance in our walk in the Light.

Think of all those famous celebrity Christians lately that have walked away from the faith. They claim to no longer be a Christian. When you look at their stories, what is usually missing? You guessed it! They don't have positive feelings for the faith such as love, joy, and peace. Maybe they once had it, but it doesn't appear to be there anymore. Think about it, how many people have you heard say "Wow, I feel so much love, joy, and peace within me from Christ, oh, I think I will leave the faith now"? I'm certain it's probably never happened! Having those types of feelings helps to confirm the reality of your faith to you as well. Experiencing positive feelings is thus a critical aspect of walking in the Light and staying in the Light.

How can you truly know that you are born again? Well, the change in your life such as with greater love, joy, and peace is part of that. We don't always walk perfectly in those things, so doubts can set in, even still. I would say another way you can know is that you're concerned about being born again. The fact that you have a desire to be born of the Spirit is a positive sign that you can look to. Another thing is to pray and meditate for an unveiling of the new creation life in you, that you would fully manifest all that there is to being born of the Spirit. Taking time to meditate on the qualities of the new life can help to strengthen them in your heart. This is but one reason why meditation is so important, as we will look at later.

FAITH AND REPENTANCE

We are all familiar with the need to have faith in Christ for salvation. Romans 10:9,10 says "that if you confess with your mouth, the Lord Jesus and believe in your heart that God has raised Him "from the dead, you will be saved. For with the heart one believes unto righteousness, and with the mouth, confession is made unto salvation" We need to understand what salvation is when we use the term. Yes, salvation is being saved from darkness or hell and being saved unto heaven. Salvation is much more than that, though. We are first and foremost saved unto God. God has redeemed us and now sets us apart for Himself. We become one with Him. Salvation is also being made whole, which is why you cease to be in darkness and are bound

11

toward a place of darkness. The brokenness due to sin sets your soul in a dark place. Now, you are being made whole in him. Now your trajectory is away from darkness and is going toward the Light. When salvation comes, you begin to move into the kingdom life and are set for a destination of the kingdom.

Faith

What does faith mean? What does belief mean? Faith is to believe in Christ and all of what he has done for us and will do for us. It's not just mental assent to belief, though. It's a trust of Christ in your life. One way of putting it is to say you embrace Christ within your being. You embrace Him at your birth and you keep embracing Him daily! The embrace of Christ goes deeper than embracing certain doctrines about Him, it involves embracing everything about Him including the essence of his being. Everything that Christ is and represents is to be fully embraced. This includes his love, compassion, kindness, forgiveness, and much more! You don't just believe in Jesus, but you take on his essence within you. So many people have certain beliefs but fail to take on his true essence, which is why they don't walk in His Light, and it is usually apparent to everyone around them whether in the church or the world.

I sometimes think in the church; we make a prayer to receive Jesus, the sum total of what it means to be a Christian, and we see what this produces. A very shallow following of Jesus, if at all. I can remember walking in this shallowness within my walk when I was younger, not understanding the full meaning of embracing Christ.

Notice that the verse speaks of confession, which can mean prayer, but also in how we speak and what we confess to ourselves within our being. Confess both in your heart and with your words the truths of God. This can include the initial prayer to receive Christ, but it also means to have a continual confession of who He is and who we are in Him. We need to constantly affirm these truths, this is where affirmations come in.

A few verses down in verse 13 it says "For "whoever calls on the name of the Lord shall be saved." If we will call upon the Lord with a genuine heart, he will save us and transform us. There really are no qualifiers placed on this verse as some might lead you to believe, the only one would be a few verses earlier that it must be heartfelt. You can trust that Christ will save you, it is his desire to do so. (I Timothy 2:4) You can call out to the Lord not just when you first become born again but may call out to be saved at any time. Your heart's desire is to be made whole, and this is partly accomplished by you crying out to Him to do this.

THE WAY

In John 14:6 it says, "Jesus said to him, "I am the way, the truth, and the life. No one comes to the Father except through Me." So we come to the Father by way of Jesus. What does Jesus being the way mean? It does mean that we come through his person, for sure, but is there more to this way than just that? Yes, to take on the way of Jesus is to embrace all that He is as we saw earlier. To embrace His love, kindness, and compassion. How this way can be expressed in a person's life can vary from time to time and circumstances to circumstance. What aspect of the way do I need right now in this moment?

Jesus also spoke of being the truth? We had seen that truth was closely connected to Light. When the Light comes, all truth is revealed and made clear. All the truths that Jesus taught are part of his truth that he gave us. All the truths about Jesus are also part of his truth that he is. The life and example that Jesus gave is a third aspect of his truth that he laid out as a foundation for us. Jesus is the truth in who He is, what He did, what He taught, and what He accomplished. To walk in the Light is to walk in Christ's truth.

Lastly, Jesus said that he was the life. Jesus' life was the supreme example, but the life that he gave on the cross was also to then give us life in a spiritual sense. We live by both his life that He lived, and by the life that He gave for us. When you embrace Christ, he also promised to give us abundant life as He says in John 10:10 "I have come that they may have life and that they may have it more abundantly." This abundant life is part of the joy, unspeakable, and peace that we gain from Christ.

THE LIGHT OF THE WORLD

God Is Light

We have been speaking of Light throughout this chapter and will do so throughout this book. The Light is a quality of being, but is it more than that? Yes, the Light is God Himself as it says in I John 1:5 "God is light and in Him is no darkness at all." Notice that not only is God the Light, but there's no darkness in Him. The Light and darkness are as far as the east is from the west. To walk in the Light is to forsake the darkness, but it's literally to walk in God, to be one with God in every conceivable way possible. You are becoming like God, hence why you are a godly man or woman. That's not just a cute saying, but a profound truth rich with meaning.

Jesus is the Light

Who else is the Light besides God? We are told in John 8:12 that Jesus is the Light as it says, "Then Jesus spoke to them again, saying, "I am the light of the world. He who follows Me shall not walk in darkness, but have the light of life." Jesus is the perfect representation of the Father in this world and is our light to see the Father's Light. Jesus told us that if we have seen Him, we have seen the Father. (John 14:9) Just as God is love (I John 4:7), so is Jesus. I have often meditated on what Jesus means and have come to see Jesus as the perfect picture of love. It's like you asked God to paint us a picture of love, and it's Jesus! We have more than some excellent teachings on love throughout scripture; we have an exact representation before us in Christ.

We Are the Light

There's a third aspect to whom the Light is. We are actually the Light of God with Christ and the Father. How is it we can become part of this Light? In Ephesians 5:14 it says, "Awake, you who sleep, Arise from the dead, And Christ will give you light". We are the Light because Christ has given it to us. Our Light flows from Him when we are born of the Spirit.

We are the Light in this world as well! Mathew 5:14 says, "You are the light of the world. A city that is set on a hill cannot be hidden". We are a part of God's Light and are becoming a more perfect representation of this Light day by day. I'm not just walking in the Light and on the path of the Light, but am actually part of the Light itself! When you begin to fully grasp that you are the Light, it can radically transform how you live this life. I become the truth in this world. I become a being of love, peace, kindness, and compassion to a world that desperately needs to see it. All that God is, all that Christ is, I am within myself. I become that ambassador for Christ that Paul spoke of. (I Corinthians 5:20). As an ambassador, I represent the King to the world, I walk in His power and authority!

JESUS IS THE SOWER OF SEEDS

Jesus tells us that He is the sower of seeds and tells how this happens. He said that some seeds fall on the roadside and the birds come and devour it. Other seeds fall into shallow soil but lack any depth, so they come up quickly and then die. A third seed is one that falls among thorns but is choked away by the thorns. The final seed is the seed that falls on good soil and produces a crop, some thirty, some sixty, and some a hundredfold. Each seed represents how a person receives the message of Christ. The first hears the word but doesn't understand it, the birds quickly take that seed away. The next seed represents someone who quickly embraces it and is excited but has no depth, so it withers away. The seed that falls among thorns is the one that allows the cares of the world to choke out his faith. The final one is the seed that truly embraces Christ and is born of the Spirit. (see Mark 13: 1-9, 18-23) Hopefully, everyone reading this book is the fourth seed and wants to have his or her seed planted deeply so that they can produce a crop within them.

Jesus Plants Multiple Seedings

One thing that I have always wondered about was whether you only get one shot at these seeds? Is it possible to have the seeds land in one of the first 3 areas the first time, but later receive the good seed that takes root? I think the answer is that Jesus does multiple seeding in people's lives. You may have gotten the first seed at one point in your life, and it made absolutely no sense to you. Maybe a few years later you heard the message again, and the experience was totally different. Maybe when you were a child, you received the second or third seed which had no root or got choked out as you got distracted by life, but later you came across the good seed. If you find yourself in one of the first 3 categories right now, I hope God will use this book to plant the good seeds in your life now. You can take time to ask God for the good seed and apply what you read in this book to help you along your path. You might also be reading this book and have received a good seed and have yielded a crop, but you really want to take your yield from a 30 to a 60 or 100. I think this book can help you as well.

The Dormant Seed

Another thing I have thought about is the person that receives Christ possibly at a young age, produces no fruit, but later in life, begins to really take hold of his faith, possibly rededicating his or her life to Christ. Does this mean they had not received a good seed earlier? It's difficult to say, but I personally believe that many children may genuinely receive Christ from a heart of love but get distracted only to come back later to Him. I would call some of these seeds dormant. They're waiting to be reactivated. This is one reason why sharing the truth about Christ is so important with children. They may go astray but may find their way back when they're older. (Proverbs 22:6) You are planting seeds in their hearts. This hits home for me because we have a seven-year-old son. We take time to have devotions and take him to programs like Awanas, a youth ministry. Maybe in your life, you had those dormant times in your walk. If your seed is dormant now, read this book and use what you learn to help activate the seed within you. The book ultimately doesn't do that, God does, but it may help point you in the right direction.

LET YOUR LIGHT SHINE

One reason we would desire to walk as children of the Light is to positively impact others around us. This starts with our family, then goes to those we interact with each day. Then it spreads to our community and ultimately the world itself. In Matthew 5:16 it says, "Let your light so shine before men, that they may see your good works and glorify your Father in heaven." As we said before, will others always see our transformation? No, but most of the time, they usually will see some change in you. Even if they don't directly see any change in you, they may be benefiting from the changes in you and because there may now be less friction, you have a better opportunity to speak to them about the things of Christ and to influence them in positive ways. They are less hostile to your life and message. You now bring more credibility, even if they don't consciously recognize it.

Often, it's not so much all the good that you do that opens the door to minister to people, it's honestly the lack of distractions from the garbage in our lives that make it possible. When you have glaring inconsistencies and flaws that scream out to people, it's hard to hear or see anything good within you.

Your transformation starts internally, which is the most important part, and then works its way outward. Your primary focus in letting your light shine should never be on the external things like I no longer smoke or go to those types of movies anymore. Your focus should also be on love and qualities that relate to love such as kindness, peace, joy, and gentleness. Basically, the Fruits of the Spirit is the starting point, but then it also moves into other qualities listed in scripture such as forgiveness, mercy, and compassion. The fruits of the Spirit are part of the fruits of repentance because as you change direction, they will be the principal things you will move toward as you advance in God Himself.

When people observe and interact with you, you may be the only witness for Christ and the things of Christ that they ever see. You want to shine forth his love as powerfully as you can. This should be your prayer and something you often meditate on. In many cases, I don't always directly meditate on my witness, but I always meditate on being a more loving person. I want to embrace all that love is and has for me. I want that to be the passion of my life, which is to fully embrace love. As I embrace love, I also embrace Christ and everything He and His Father are about.

PICK UP YOUR CROSS

Jesus taught his disciples in Matthew 16:24 to pick up their cross to follow Him as it says "Then Jesus said to His disciples, "If anyone desires to come after Me, let him deny himself, and take up his cross, and follow Me. "We need to pick up our cross daily to follow Him. When we think of picking up our cross, we think of sacrificing for Him as well as suffering for Him. We also think of dying to our selfish ways. All of this is true, but really, how do you do this? This may tempt many to go looking for ways to deny what they want and find ways to make their life miserable to say that they are suffering and sacrificing for Christ. This can lead to a fleshly esoteric following of Jesus that misses the mark.

The best way to die to selfishness isn't to directly focus on our selfishness and start giving things up left and right. This may seem counterintuitive to some. When you do this, you often end up becoming self-righteous and judgmental. This has been exhibited throughout history, and we can see believers who still fall into this trap today. The real way to die to selfishness is to be immersed in His love, peace, and joy each day. Think of it as being born again each day. You start each day fresh and new with God and have an opportunity to become a new creation each day. Yes, you had one day probably way back that started your spiritual journey, but you seek to live and bathe in being born of his Spirit. Some churches speak of a second blessing. Other churches speak of the Baptism of the Holy Spirit being a second event. It's really not that Baptism is a separate event from your new birth or that you receive only a second blessing, rather, it's a continual blessing daily that you should seek. It's a continual immersion in his love that you should seek. Yes, as you immerse yourself daily, you will reach new heights in your walk and may see God move in more powerful ways, but our experiences with God aren't limited to a day or a second event but are for life and are always in the now.

We do need to yield to the Spirit, and the primary way we yield is by living in His love. God may call you to do this or that or to give up something, but if you are walking in His love and Light, the changes that do need to happen will flow more naturally, they will feel effortless. Love and peace from Him will change your desires as well, so He may not even need to say "stop doing this or that" or "go do this or that". You will find yourself moving in that direction. I can attest to this, I can remember trying to stop watching movies with sex and violence because I knew it was the "right thing", not because I actually wanted to do this. It was a struggle and a work of the flesh. Once you immerse yourself in love, however, the desire is gone. You may actually be repulsed but such violence and promiscuous sex in movies and TV.

Your Light will shine more brightly when you seek His kingdom. As Mathew 6:33 says "But seek first the kingdom of God and his righteousness, and all these things will be added to you." (ESV) Since we know what his Kingdom is, that of love, peace, righteousness, and joy, then you know how to seek his Kingdom each day. It's no longer a mystery. Press into love, joy, and peace, and anything connected with love. It's really that simple.

GOD'S LOVE IS NEW EVERYDAY

We should seek God each day because God has something new to give us each day. As Lamentations says in 3:22, 23 "Because of the Lord's great love we are not consumed, for his compassion never fail. They are new every morning; great is your faithfulness." This goes along with being born of the Spirit each day. He has more love and compassion to shower on us each day, really in each moment. Each day with God can be a new beginning for you, even if yesterday or the last few weeks and months have been terrible. Maybe you haven't been walking in His love, but you can start over again. His love was always there, but you were distracted by so many other things. It could have been sorrow, depression, or the cares of this world. You can not only take each day to start fresh, but even each moment, I've often had to do that when I find myself getting up and reacting in anger. Let the past go and live in this present moment in Him.

Notice that the passage says that what God has for us is "new every morning". I think it is so important to start your day with God in some way. You don't necessarily have to have a full devotion with Him for an hour and meditate on Him at that time. You could start with a few minutes of prayer and do affirmations of who you are in Him and what you're grateful for. I start this even before I get out of bed. I will pray about things going on in my life and thank Him for a few minutes. I then get moving and do affirmations for about 10 minutes while I do things. So many great things you can affirm such as "I'm the Light of this world", often I shorten it to "I am Light". You could do affirmations for love, peace, beauty, etc. We will get into affirmations more fully later in this book.

You should also close your day with Him as well. You can

pray, do affirmations, read a devotion, or a portion of scripture. I do meditation in the middle of the day, which takes about 45 minutes. This is a time where I meditate on anything related to God which could be a scripture or the Fruits of the Spirit.

I love how it says because of God's great love; we aren't consumed. Why would we be consumed? It would be due to sin which propels us into darkness. If His love prevents that, then love is clearly more powerful than sin. This is why the focal point of walking in the Light is love and NOT avoiding sin. We focus on what gives us power and not on what takes it away from us. This is much of what the book of Romans is about, the law itself which tells you what sin is but will never make you holy. It is faith or the embrace of Christ, and to embrace Christ is to embrace love.

God's compassion never fails, we don't have to despair about sin in our life; we need to embrace his compassion and walk in compassion. Compassion is one of the great attributes of His love. Compassion has the potential to change virtually everything in your life, and it certainly can change your perspective on how you see others. When you have compassion, forgiveness becomes much easier to do. Compassion is closely related to empathy. Once you can empathize with someone who has wronged you and why they may have wronged you, then you can let it go.

GOD GIVES BENEFITS EACH DAY

God wants to give us blessings each and every day. I love what it says in Psalms 68:19 "Blessed be the Lord, who daily loadeth us with benefits, even the God of our salvation. Selah." (KJV) What a powerful statement,Heloads us with benefits every day! We should always seek to be in His love daily, but according to his verse,Heautomatically showers us with gifts each day whether we recognize it or not. Everything you have is given to you at your new birth, everything you need is supplied to you each day which enables you to fully walk as a child of the Light. It may not always seem like this is true, but as you go into his Presence day by day, moment by moment, this truth will become more apparent to you within your spirit.

MY PERSONAL JOURNEY

Everything I wrote about in this chapter and this entire book reflects what I've learned and experienced walking in the Light. I came to Christ at 9 at a summer day camp for blind and low vision kids. I have a visual impairment, which I've had since birth. An older boy named Darrell was sharing Christ with me on the swings. I was hesitant at first but felt led to receive Jesus. I prayed to ask Christ into my heart and so started my journey in the Light. I can remember a few weeks later being on the summer camp bus and doing something that I knew I shouldn't. I heard a voice within me say "You're a Christian now, you can't do that". I knew from that point on, everything in my life would be different. It wasn't all at once, but I had started my adventure of faith.

Soon thereafter, my older sister Janet moved back home. She had recently come to Christ as well. We started attending Calvary Chapel Costa Mesa, a well-known mega-church in Southern California. We really enjoyed it and loved borrowing cassette tapes from the tape lending library to listen to messages by Chuck Smith and other Calvary pastors. This was in the early 1980s. Though I absolutely couldn't wait to hear a tape with Janet, the application of most of what was taught would come much later. I think listening to all those sermons and going to Calvary helped to plant seeds in me, that though they laid dormant at times, would eventually spring to life by God in due time. My overall knowledge of the faith was grounded in these times.

I remember going forward many times to rededicate my life to Christ when an altar call would be given because I knew I was flawed and always wanted to draw closer to Christ. I really didn't understand what repentance was or that just "asking for forgiveness" didn't capture what it meant to walk in His Light. At times, my faith was shallow, lacking true depth.

As I got older, legalism would sometimes set in. I can remember intentionally deciding to not go to R-rated movies or drink alcohol. The alcohol was easy, I hate the taste of it. Even though I don't hold to such legalism today. I don't drink simply because of the taste, nor do I generally go to R-rated movies, because I find so much of what is in them to be repulsive within my spirit. At one point in my life, I got into following the dietary laws for a few years, which was an odd chapter in my life. I've since let all of those legalisms go. These legalisms had led me into a judgmental spirit.

I remember times of seeking to have the perfect doctrine and wondering if any church had the perfect doctrine, or at least came closer to it than any other church out there. Ironically, by focusing so intently on perfect doctrine, it caused me to pursue all winds of doctrine as the scripture speaks of. (see Ephesians 4:14) I got into various forms of hyper-grace, for example.

Several years ago, God started moving me away from my doctrinaire way of thinking into simply focusing on living in love. This includes the qualities of love such as the fruits of the Spirit as well as compassion, mercy, and forgiveness to mention a few. This opened my eyes as to what true repentance was and how to actually walk in the Light. All this transformation led up to my dream in February 2021 of walking as children of the Light which inspired the writing of this book. When I say, I'm no longer doctrinaire, it doesn't mean I hold to no doctrines or don't have any interest in theology, but it's not my focal point. The word doctrine means teaching, so if you follow the teachings of Christ in love, for example, you're holding to a doctrine. Since making love my focal point, it has revolutionized my life. One of the main ways I changed my focus was due to meditation, as we will get to in chapter 3.

Application

1. Think back to the time when you first received Christ to be born again. What was the experience like? What was going on around you? Were you pressured by a preacher or parents to go forward? Did the person sharing Christ literally scare the "hell" out of you? Write down this experience in your journal. Now, think about what you wish would have possibly been different. Could they have emphasized some of the things I mentioned above, such as being immersed in His love, peace, and joy? Could they have done something differently? If you can't think of a time where you made a commitment to Christ specifically, pray now that God would make you born of His Spirit and shower you with His love, peace, and joy. Commit to walking in His Light and love for the rest of your life, you can start this journey of walking as a child of the Light with everyone else reading this right now!

2. Take a few minutes to think about what your spiritual journey has been like since you embraced Christ. Write down your experience. Did you have any dormant times? Did you ever fall into legalism or stray from the faith? What are some key things you've learned in your journey? If you embraced Christ through reading this chapter, what do you believe led you to the point of deciding to come to Christ? Did God use anyone or any circumstances to help lead to this point today? Write down your experience in your journal.

3. Commit for the next 3 weeks to pray first thing in the morning and just before you go to bed at night. If you already do this, great. Make sure to focus your prayers on things of the Spirit such as love, joy, peace, patience, kindness, goodness, faithfulness, gentleness, and self-control.

4. Write down a list of at least 10 things you are grateful for that God has given you. Connect them to qualities of love, joy, peace, and generosity. From that list, create short affirmations that you say to yourself to remind you of God's goodness. If you mentioned your family, you might say "I love my family, they

are a gift". If it's your health, you might affirm "I'm blessed with excellent health". You should say each affirmation at least 10 times each. A good place to do this is just after your morning and evening prayers.

2. PRAY WITHOUT CEASING

"pray without ceasing" (I Thessalonians 5:17)

I think most Christians know that prayer is one of the most important steps to being a disciple of Christ and really walking as a child in the Light. Even knowing this, many of us neglect our prayer lives with God. To truly walk in the Light and be Light to the world, you're going to have to commit to praying consistently every day. I give suggestions throughout this chapter and book, it's a matter of being dedicated to prayer that will be necessary. Prayer is your lifeline to God that helps you to live the Christian life. If you fail to tap into this lifeline, you will not grow in Him as you should. Prayer is one of the main ways you also build your relationship with Him. It's your chance to talk to God and express what you're going through. It's your time to thank and praise Him. It's your time to commune with Him. You can't build any relationship without communication. If you didn't talk to your spouse for days on end or only a few minutes a day, how would your relationship be? Not a strong one.

Prayer is not only a way to build a relationship with God, but really, it's a way to build a relationship with other people, as we shall see. Prayer is also important for your own life, health, and well-being.

POWER OF PRAYER

We have all been taught that there is power in prayer, but is it actually true? In Matthew 21:21, 22 we read "So Jesus answered and said to them, "Assuredly, I say to you, if you have faith and do not doubt, you will not only do what was done to the fig tree but also if you say to this mountain, 'Be removed and be cast into the sea,' it will be done. And whatever things you ask in prayer, believing, you will receive." Is prayer really about moving literal mountains? Most would quickly recognize that prayer isn't about literal mountains and fig trees, but about moving the obstacles in our life. It's about walking in the power of God. It's about praying for everything in our lives that concerns us and praying for others that we love and care for. It's about praying for those in the community and world that we don't even know. It's about transforming our hearts and lives. We want to remove any obstacles in the way and see the power of God move in all areas of life and our world.

We by faith believe in the power of God to move in prayer, but is there actually any evidence that prayer does in fact work? We know times we prayed or others prayed, and the prayer doesn't seem to have been answered. Hopefully, we also have times where we or others prayed, and they do appear to have been answered. I believe all prayers are answered but according to His will. If it was a person's time to go, they may still die even though people prayed for him or her. A person may need to go through a trial to grow or be pointed to where he or she needs to be. God may answer your prayers even though they may not always be in the way you asked or thought you wanted it answered. He may be showing grace, mercy, or love even when it's not obvious to us. The person dying may be going to heaven. A trial might build character in the person going through it, or it might be the push to get the help he or she needs.

All of this is well and good. Prayer is always for our best interest or the interest of the other person according to His will, but is there any evidence that prayer is really working? Yes, there is actually scientific evidence that prayer can make a difference that has been objectively shown to be the case.

One study in 1999 of hospital cardiac patients in St. Luke's in Kansas City, Missouri demonstrated that prayer can make a difference. A group of 1,000 patients were in the study. 500 were prayed for and 500 were not. The prayer was for a speedy recovery, with no complications. With cardiac patients, there can be a whole host of complications that can happen, including things such as chest pains, pneumonia, infection, and death. The volunteers were all Christians and were only given the first name of the patient to pray for. The patients were prayed daily for 4 weeks. The patients were never told that they were being prayed for, nor were they ever visited by the volunteers. The prayer given was known as intercessory prayer. The study concluded that those prayed for fared 11% better in terms of complications, which was statistically significant.[1]

In another study in 1988, patients were prayed for by volunteers who also did not contact the patients, and the patients didn't know they were being prayed for. The prayer was for a faster recovery. In that study, there was a marked difference in how fast the patients were released from the hospital. The patients prayed for had quicker recoveries and were able to be released sooner than those not prayed for.[2]

What is the point of discussing these studies? To demonstrate to you that prayer does in fact have power. These are cases you can see and are documented. It helps to prove that God is at work and responds to our prayers, even if we don't always see it. We can start from a position of knowing that prayer does work and makes a difference. We aren't wasting our time no matter how it may look in a particular circumstance. We may not know how God works, or why He does whatHedoes, but there is a clear metaphysical reality to prayer demonstrated ironically by science itself.

COMMUNION WITH GOD

Prayer allows you to enter into communion with God in a profound way. God's desire is to become one with us and commune with us in our souls. In Revelation 3:20 we read, "Behold, I stand at the door and knock. If anyone hears My voice and opens the door, I will come in to him and dine with him, and he with Me". We often hear this verse used when sharing the gospel with people to invite Christ into their lives. I think it's a wonderful verse to use for that purpose, but I think it has more applications than just that. We who are already believers can take this verse as an invitation to communion with God daily and one of the most important ways to do this through prayer. I love howHeuses the allegory of coming in and dining with us. Eating a meal with someone in scripture was one of the principal ways you fellowship with others. Today in our own culture this is still much the same case. To share a meal together is an intimate way to fellowship with someone. Communion in the New Testament was often connected with a fellowship meal. (I Corinthians 11). Sharing a meal can take place in a variety of settings, home, restaurant, convention hall, church, etc. The fact that Jesus is seeking to dine within your home is significant. He's not seeking to meet you in some distant strange place but to enter the door or your heart. The early church often took communion in homes (Acts 2:46).

Prayer is a uniquely spiritual communion with God. In Psalms 145:18 it says "The Lord is near to all who call on him, to all who call on him in truth." (NIV) Prayer draws God close to you in a way that very few things can do. If you want God to be near to you, prayer is one of the best go-tos you have in your spiritual toolkit. James 4:8 says "Draw near to God, and he will draw near to you." (ESV) As you draw toward God's Light in prayer, it draws Him to you. He doesn't just force Himself on you but seeks those who embrace Him. Was there ever a time in your prayers when you felt such intimacy? Maybe you were going through a crisis in your life. You can have this intimacy anytime and not just when you're suffering or in trouble.

CONNECTION WITH OTHERS

Prayer can not only bring communion with God but it can connect us to other people. There's a connection when you pray with others in fellowship. I can remember having a deep fellowship at prayer meetings with other believers. I had times like this in high school and college bible studies as well as weekly prayer meetings at church when I would attend them. The bond was often made stronger when we would all pray while holding hands. Can you remember a close intimacy with other believers when you were praying with them? Consider trying to find times when you can pray with others, whether at a formal meeting or just informally. Even praying over meals with your family can help to bring you closer together.

Prayer can also help to create greater connections for the people you are praying for. It keeps them in your mind and heart. It helps you to direct attention away from just your own issues and toward the needs of others. Prayer can help to propel you to serve others. It's the starting point for service, sometimes that's all we can do in some situations. Sometimes it's all we can do for that other person, is to pray for them. As we pray, it can soften our hearts and move the energy of God in both their direction as well as our own.

Prayer can not only create a stronger connection to other people but can help to put our hearts at one with them. As Jesus prayed in John 17:21 "that they all may be one, as You, Father, *are* in Me, and I in You; that they also may be one in Us, that the world may believe that You sent Me." Prayer makes us one with each other but also one with God together in unity.

Part of this oneness that is created between fellow believers in prayer and with God is the fact that prayer places God in our midst, as it says in Matthew 18:20 "For where two or three are gathered together in My name, I am there in the midst of them." Prayer is a true element of what it means to be the church or called out ones. The church isn't a building but a unity of believers with one of the main ways uniting us being prayer.

How can we change the world? No better way is to become one with other people, which prayer does, just as it brings us into oneness with God. When millions of believers begin to walk in a deeper oneness, strongholds will fall, the mountains that divide us can suddenly start to come falling down, to be buried in a sea of transformation. When you begin to walk in greater oneness through prayer, your perspective on how you view others will begin to radically change. The more you pray, the more you can become one with others.

FEEL THE LOVE

One of the strongest reasons to pray is that love is manifested within us. This love is present in every way conceivable and runs in many directions. The expressions of love can take a whole host of forms. The seeds of love which were planted at our spiritual birth are now given time to germinate and grow within our heart and mind. Besides the love growing within our hearts, God can and often does give you a special impartation of love when you pray. Just be open to receiving it. This is one way to continually be immersed in His Spirit, which we talked about in the first chapter. Prayer puts you in a state for this flow of his Spirit in your life.

When you commune with God in prayer, love is one of the many things produced from such a union. You grow in your love for Him, and you feel the love you have for Him grows within you. You can start to feel and walk in His love more powerfully. This love will help to keep you close to Him and walk in His ways, which is the essence of walking as a child of the Light. Your spirit is one with Him in this love.

How do you produce the Fruits of the Holy Spirit in your life? One of the best ways is to pray. When you pray, you can begin to produce fruits of love and those qualities associated with love, such as kindness, peace, joy, and gentleness. His Spirit is the one that produces them, but He allows you to aid Him in this process. Think of it much like a child helping her grandfather

31

plant flowers in the garden. You are being given the opportunity to produce things of beauty with God within your own being!

You not only grow in your love for God, but your love for others can begin to expand. As you pray with others, you experience greater love for those partners in prayer. This can be those in your spiritual family as well as those in your literal household. You will grow in love as you begin to pray for other people as well. It's good to pray for the world and your nation in a general sense. I do that often in my own prayers, but always make sure you take some of your time in prayer to pray for specific people. Pray for those you currently love and care about. Pray for those you don't know well or have any strong feelings about. Yes, pray for your enemies or just those people that may not be your enemies but have a way of getting under your skin!

Increasing your love in prayer is the primary way that you can feel connected to others in your life and even those not in your life. You can know that the love is deepening and growing as you pray for other people. You may find yourself feeling the love for these other people. No, we don't pray just to get the warm fuzzies but it's a wonderful feeling to have! I love to feel the connection in my heart and to feel the love welling up within my being. As time goes by, I actually feel the love itself more and more, it's daily for me rather than just occasionally. Start praying where you are, and you will feel the love more and more each day. It does take time, just like planting a tree doesn't grow overnight.

One thing to focus on during your prayer time is how much God loves you and other people. As it says in Psalms 117:2 "For great is his steadfast love toward us, and the faithfulness of the Lord endures forever. Praise the Lord!" (ESV) The Psalms is replete with his love as it also says in Psalms 136:1 "Give thanks to the Lord, for he is good, for his steadfast love endures forever." God's love is great, and it never ends! He loves you just asHeloves every other person on the face of the planet and every person who has ever lived. Think of the worst person you can think of, and God loves them more than you love your own child! Take time in prayer to recognize His love for you and others. As you begin to really recognize His love in prayer, it can change how you perceive others. It may feel awkward to thank God for His love, but eventually, you will get it. Thank God for all the ways He loves you, including loving you with all your failings and shortcomings. This can change how you view yourself as well.

PRAY FOR COMPASSION

Another way you connect to people in prayer is by expanding with compassion. Prayer can bring compassion for other people and their suffering that they may be going through. As you pray specifically for those suffering, you will feel compassion growing inside you just as your love grows. You take time to pray for those that are sick or not feeling well. You pray for those that are going through emotional trauma or depression. Sometimes it might be just praying for someone who's feeling a little down that day. You pray for those that are suffering with bitterness, guilt, shame, or any other negative emotions. You can grow in compassion but also send compassion to them in prayer. This may be all they need or at least go a long way in helping them. What I've started to do is when anyone asks me to pray for them because they're going through something difficult, is to pray for them right then and there. Whether it's with them or silently in my mind and heart. I also try to stop and pray for someone I see suffering in some way immediately. Don't wait to pray! Pray right then and send compassion to them and build it within you. Also, if you're like me, if you wait till it's your "official" prayer time, there is a good chance you will have forgotten about it. You might want to write it down to pray for later, but still, pray right on the spot too.

Prayer isn't the stopping point for showing and growing in compassion, of course, it is the starting point, and in many cases, it may be all we can do for that person in the moment.

It's a powerful practice though, so don't disparage prayer for compassion. Prayer is one of the easiest ways to start walking as a child of the Light and grow in your compassion. Seek to make compassion a focal point of prayer.

Compassion in prayer is not limited to other people. You can pray for yourself, which can lead to more compassion for yourself. Some might belittle the idea of "needing" compassion for yourself but if you want to walk as a child of the Light, everything needed in this world begins with you, including compassion. If you lack compassion for yourself, it's more difficult to have it for others. If you can grow in compassion for yourself, it will spill over into other people in most cases. Notice I say compassion for yourself, not pity. We don't want a pity party, but we want to feel love and compassion for ourselves and at times just give ourselves a break emotionally.

Compassion is not limited to humans either. You can grow in compassion for even animals with prayer. Have you ever prayed for a sick pet or someone's sick pet? Have you ever prayed for someone who has lost a pet? I can remember being at a prayer meeting when a woman wanted prayer for her cat, but she asked if that would be OK. The message to her had been sent that prayer for an animal may not be worthy of God's time. Nothing could be further from the truth. Jesus even told us he cares for the birds of the air. (Mathew 6:26-34). Part of walking as a child of the Light has to include compassion for animals. In Proverbs 12:10 it says, "A righteous *man* regards the life of his animal,". There is a connection between animal cruelty and those that go on to harm other people.[3] Might there also be a connection between those that show compassion for animals and human beings? I think the answer may be yes?

What about our compassion for God? I believe that even our compassion for God can increase as we pray, which can help us from straying from Him as some have done recently. When your compassion for God increases, things like bitterness toward God diminish. The compassionate heart starts with compassion for our creator first and foremost.

Compassion like love is one of those qualities that have the potential to change the world. Think of anyone who you believe to be a compassionate person. Who are those well-known who come to mind as having compassionate hearts? Two people that come to my mind are Mother Teresa and Mr. Rogers. That may sound funny, but I think most would agree that these two individuals represented what compassion looks like to the world. Ironically, they both worked primarily with children. Compassion for a child and instilling compassion in children is so important to creating a better world. One thing I know that both Mother Teresa and Mr. Rogers did was to pray. They were both earnestly praying people. Most may not know that Mr. Rogers was a minister and that his ministry within his church was to children with his show. Both would agree, I believe, that one of the most important ways we can increase our compassion is through prayer. Do you think this world would be a better place if millions more had a compassionate heart like Mother Teresa and Mr. Rogers had? I think the answer is an overwhelming yes![4]

We can actually pray for compassion in prayer and are instructed to seek compassion as it says in Colossians 3:12 "Put on then, as God's chosen ones, holy and beloved, compassionate hearts, kindness, humility, meekness, and patience," (ESV). We put on the qualities listed above through prayer. You gain compassion as you pray, but you can also directly ask for compassion and every other quality. In the verse, it speaks of being a chosen one, chosen for what? We are actually elected or chosen to walk in love, kindness, patience, and meekness, or gentleness, that's part of our mission here on earth. We are all called to this. Unfortunately, not all are responding at this present time.

PRAY FOR EMPATHY

As you pray for others and with others, you develop both sympathy and empathy. What is the difference between the two? With both, you're able to relate to people's pain and struggles. Sympathy understands how the person feels. Empathy experiences how the person feels. Both correlate to compassion and grow out of compassion. Compassion comes from a general kind, caring heart for others.[5] Now, you're specifically focused on a particular person. Empathy and sympathy are an intimate level of connection with the other person. If you can develop compassion, you can then sympathize with another person. As you begin to sympathize, you can then begin to empathize to actually feel their pain. Prayer, along with meditation, can make it possible to experience the other person's emotions. Maybe God reminds you of similar instances in your life. It could also be that God places on you the actual emotions, which is difficult to explain and is a bit metaphysical. I've actually experienced the emotions of others in prayer and mediation. You can even ask God to let you experience within your soul what the other person is feeling so that you can better understand them. People who have had life reviews during a near-death experience have reported feeling everything that caused others both physically, emotionally, and spiritually. They may also experience pain in what the other person went through to help them understand why the person is the way they are.[6] So our judgment at the end of this life is partially a giant empathy learning session. Why not do this now with prayer and meditation?

In Ephesians 6:2 Paul says to "Bear one another's burdens, and so fulfill the law of Christ." The first place to bear the other person's burden is in prayer. To bear is to take on, so it's more than just being supportive. You want to experience their burdens with them so you can come alongside them in their need. In this, you fulfill the law of Christ. What is the law of Christ? Jesus commanded us to love one another in John 13:34 "A new commandment I give to you, that you love one another; as I have loved you". Empathy, like compassion, is an aspect of love. Love is like a diamond with many facets in it.

To be able to empathize with where a person is and why they may have done what they did is the first step to letting go of judgments. In prayer, you can speak to God and express to Him how you are feeling in a situation and pray for that other person. You can then ask for a greater understanding of why the person may have done what they did. Such prayers can allow you to better "Judge not, that you be not judged." (Mathew 7:1)

When you can empathize with an enemy or a person you're upset with, then forgiveness becomes easy. This is why Jesus said in Matthew 5:44 "But I say to you, love your enemies, bless those who curse you, do good to those who hate you, and pray for those who spitefully use you and persecute you". To love your enemy will take forgiveness and prayer opens the door for forgiveness to happen.

Does prayer actually make you more forgiving? The answer is yes, in fact, one study demonstrated that people feel more forgiving toward their spouse or friend and let things go faster when they regularly pray for them. Science backs up prayer as a path to forgiveness, which is so important to improving relationships with family and friends as well as those we come into contact with each day. Think about how this could help you at work or school as well. Greater forgiveness is vital to walking as a child of the Light.[7]

PRAYER OPENS UP GRATITUDE

One of the main things to pray about during your prayer time is to thank God for what He has given you in your life. Every time you pray, a significant portion of your time should be focused on gratitude. In Psalms 9:1 It says "I will give thanks to you, Lord, with all my heart". (NIV). The more you spend time thanking God for all He has blessed you within your life, the more grateful you will actually feel in your life. You could even take time to write down all the things you are grateful for in your life and then take that list into your prayers. "God thank you for my family" and then list individual people within your family. "Thank you for my good health", then list out things about your health that are good specifically. Maybe you just got a report that your blood pressure is good, thank Him for that. If you simply feel good, thank Him for that.

Developing an attitude of gratefulness in your prayer life can completely change your mindset. You will become more positive and hopeful. You can sometimes use times to pray about what you're grateful for when you need to be reminded of what you have in your life that is good. This can help to lighten your mood when you're down.

Gratefulness can help to defeat many negative emotions, such as bitterness, envy, and greed. It can help to keep you from throwing those pity parties we mentioned earlier. It can help you to love God more easily and others as well. Gratefulness gives you a more hopeful perspective on life. Having a grateful heart is an important way that you will be able to walk as a child of the Light.

PRAYER CAN REFOCUS YOU

In this crazy, chaotic world that is constantly changing without a moment's notice, we can all become overwhelmed. Even the most spiritually mature among us. This is why prayer is so critical to walking the spiritual path. Prayer can help to focus us on the things of God rather than the things of this world. Prayer can also help to refocus our mind and heart on Him. We so easily become distracted and start to react from a place of stress, anger, fear, pride, lust, and a host of other negative emotions. We can lose sight of His love, peace, and joy in a split second. This is why we need to constantly be refocusing ourselves through prayer. The verse for this chapter is "Pray without ceasing". (I Thessalonians 5:17) We should have a habit of praying throughout the day. If you don't have that, seek to develop it. You can pray about anything, for the light to change, for someone who is going to an important meeting. You can pray during a downtime moment. Be constantly looking for moments to pray.

We as believers are to have vigilance in our prayer life, as it says in Ephesians 6:18 "praying always with all prayer and supplication in the Spirit, being watchful to this end with all perseverance and supplication for all the saints" Get in the habit of praying about anything and everything and especially for those you love. You should have regular times of prayer, but also seek to pray for things informally as you go through your day.

Within Judaism, the Jews have three times a day that they formally enter into prayer. You should have formal times where you sit down and take time to pray specifically during your day. These are not the only times to pray, but this is your primary focus at these times. As I have mentioned, I am in the habit of praying first thing in the morning in bed or when I get out of bed. I also pray when I'm going to bed at night. I do my affirmations after my prayer time. To do that would get you praying in the morning and at night. Then if you could find a few minutes sometime in the afternoon, that would be valuable as well. If you don't already, start to pray over meals whether you're alone, silently, or with the family out loud. Make prayer one of your priorities in the day. This will keep your mind on Christ and allow you to better walk as a child of the Light.

PRAYER CAN LIFT YOUR BURDENS

We all carry around so many burdens in our life. They may be emotional, spiritual, family, financial, or physical. Sometimes it feels like we have the weight of the world on our shoulders. If you are married and have kids, you may understand this well. How do we release these burdens from us? There're several ways, such as meditation and prayer. Prayer is one of the easiest and most effective ways to let it go.

To not be overwhelmed and stressed, we all need ways to

decompress during the day. Prayer is a way to decompress. Think of praying to God as talking over your problems with your best friend or the greatest therapist, becauseHereally is both things and much more. Sometimes just being able to talk things out can be cathartic in itself. We also know that God cares for us and is powerful enough to change how we feel and the situation within His will.

Do you want to let your anxiety go? Then pray as it says in Philippians 4:6, 7 "Do not be anxious about anything, but in every situation, by prayer and petition, with thanksgiving, present your requests to God. And the peace of God, which transcends all understanding, will guard your hearts and your minds in Christ Jesus." (NIV) In prayer, our hearts and minds are guarded against stress and anxiety. Our problems are really his problems. Give them over to God and stop worrying about them!

God actually encourages us to unburden ourselves with Him. In I Peter 5:7 it says "And cast all your cares on God, for he takes care of you." (Aramaic Bible in Plain English). In another translation, it says to leave your worries with Him "Leave all your worries with Him, because He cares for you." (Good News Translation). We can just leave those bags at His throne. He's got us covered. Notice it says that He cares for us, this is why we can bring them to Him. He cares for us both as a person, but He also cares about what concerns us, which is comforting to know.

PRAYER CAN IMPROVE YOUR MENTAL AND PHYSICAL HEALTH

We've seen that prayer can help you be more compassionate, loving, grateful, and forgiving. Many of us know all this from personal experience. Prayer can also help to improve your overall mental and physical health. This isn't just a feeling that we have or based solely on our own experience or the experiences of others we know but is what the science actually says as well. Many studies have shown that prayer has many of the same benefits as meditation and yoga. We will cover the importance of meditation in the next chapter. Prayer helps to actively lower stress and anxiety.[8] Maybe this is why the scriptures instruct us to be anxious for nothing but to go to prayer with our concerns. (Philippians 4:6, 7). God knew from the beginning what science is now demonstrating when it comes to relieving anxiety in our lives. Prayer is not only good for the soul, but for the mind and body. Prayer serves both the people being prayed for, but also the one praying. We can cast our cares on Him and KNOW that it will truly make a difference.

With the reduction of stress and anxiety, this translates into "better physiological functioning," such as lower levels of the stress hormone cortisol, lower blood pressure, and improved immune functioning. In today's world, anything that can help to improve your immune system is a good thing.

In addition to lowering stress and anxiety, studies have also shown that prayer can help people with mental illness to recover faster.[9] If prayer can help people recover from mental illness, might it also help to prevent or reduce the onslaught of mental illness in the first place? I believe the answer may be a yes. We have great compassion for those that suffer from mental illness, but with prayer, we have the ability to lower the incidents of mental illness and can help the world move into a much better place.

One thing that is critical that we've already mentioned with prayer is the frequency, which is important in fully reaping the benefits. Occasional prayer will never get you to the place you hopefully want to be walking in the Light. Studies also show that to specifically benefit mentally from prayer, it has to be with some frequency.

Our primary focus in prayer is to help others and be the Light for others, but part of walking in the Light is showing love toward ourselves. If recognizing that prayer can benefit your own health, it may be one more reason that motivates you to pray each day and pray throughout the day.

A GENUINE HEART

Besides praying consistently and frequently, praying from a sincere heart is critical to experiencing a transformed life and walking in the Light. As Hebrews 10:22 says, "let us draw near to God with a sincere heart and with the full assurance that faith brings, having our hearts sprinkled to cleanse us from a guilty conscience and having our bodies washed with pure water." (NIV) God wants us to pray from the heart of faith and love. When there's depth to your prayers, they move the heart of God in your direction. It's from a genuine heart that you embrace Him, and it's out of the same heart that you should seek to pray to Him each day. There is a real energy or power released from a prayer prayed from the depths of our hearts. It touches us and God in profound ways. God wants you to pray with your entire being, which includes your heart. You may have felt God more strongly when you were crying out to God with a heavy heart and experienced this truth firsthand. The deeper the prayer, the higher it ascends to His throne room. The more shallow the prayer, the more likely it doesn't leave the ceiling.

Notice that praying out of a sincere heart has a purifying effect on you. It helps to wash away a guilty conscience and helps us to even feel better within our bodies. So often, we live with guilt and shame because of what we may have said or done in the past. If we take these things to God from a contrite heart, we can feel the release from them. Guilt and shame have a way of holding us down spiritually. It's like trying to swim with weights on your legs. These weights will hinder our ability to walk as children in the Light.

God also wants us to pray in faith, believing that He will move on our behalf. As Mark 11:24 says, "Therefore I say to you, whatever things you ask when you pray, believe that you receive them, and you will have them." Trust that God is hearing your prayer and will answer it, even if He doesn't answer it the way you expect Him to. Have faith that it will work out perfectly according to His will in His timing. Some prayers may take years or decades to be fulfilled but stick with it!

MY EXPERIENCE WITH PRAYER

I have personally experienced everything I've written about prayer in my life at different times. I've experienced greater communion with God and connection to others whom I was praying with or praying for. I've felt waves of love, compassion, empathy, joy, and peace in prayer. I don't always feel these emotions, but often I do. I would love to tell you that since becoming a Christian, I've had a consistent and committed prayer life. Probably like many reading this, I've had times where my consistency and commitment was strong and other times in my life, not so much. My meditation times have actually pushed me to be more consistent with other areas of my walk, such as prayer. When you recommend people to sit down at a set time each day to pray for a certain period of time, many will do it for a while but most will usually fall away from it.

I've honestly found that making prayer simple and informal can be the easiest way to make sure prayer is a part of your life. You can have formal sessions in the day, I think you should. I've gotten in the habit of praying a few minutes before I get out of bed in the morning and when I first get in bed at night. If I forget in the morning, and I realize it, I will just pray silently as I go about my day. Praying over meals is also a good way to incorporate prayer into your life. Try to stop and pray anytime something concerning comes up in the day or to thank God for something you find enjoyment in during the day, such as a sunny day. Make prayer as natural as you can. To add depth, try to feel and think about what you're praying for or about. If you're praying for someone hurting, ponder their pain for a few seconds and try to understand what they're really going through. If you're thanking God for the people you love in your life, try to ponder how much you love them and why. This will add more heart and earnestness to your prayers.

Application

1. Pull out your journal. List all the people in your life that you love specifically. Write down their names and try to come up with at least five things that you love about them. Do the same with God. What are at least five things you love about God? Now, here is a more difficult one. Think of five things you love about yourself. Take this list and try to praise and thank God for everyone listed that you love, as well as the reasons why you love them. Allow yourself to really feel the love that you have for them as you pray for them. Make sure to include God and yourself in these prayers.

2. Can you think of anyone that is suffering or going through a rough time right now? Write down at least three people you can think of. What specifically could they use to help them in their suffering? Be as specific with this list as you can for your journal. Take these people into your prayers for the next week and really try to imagine what they're going through. Imagine how you would feel in such a situation. This will help to create more compassion within you.

3. Is there anyone who you would consider your enemy today? Is there anyone that maybe isn't an enemy but has a way of just getting under your skin? This can be a loved one at times. Write down these names in your journal. Write down what bothers you about them. Write down why they may be the way they are, but try to come up with reasons not infused with personal judgments like "because they're a nasty person". Take these people into your prayers over the next week and pray for them in detail. Pray that God would allow you to empathize with them and forgive them. Pray that He would help you release any bitterness or anger.

3. MEDITATE ON THESE THINGS

"Finally, brethren, whatever things are true, whatever things are noble, whatever things are just, whatever things are pure, whatever things are lovely, whatever things are of good report, if there is any virtue and if there is anything praiseworthy—meditate on these things." (Philippians 4:8)

We have so many tools to aid us in walking as a child of the Light. In some cases, they can all be helpful at any given moment. In other cases, a specific tool may be needed to help us move forward. In many respects, they're like pieces to a puzzle that when they come together, they complete the picture of our spiritual walk. Many people have missing pieces, and they fail to fully walk in the Light as they should. It's also like the many facets of a diamond. We want to let each facet shine through to display the beauty of the spiritual diamond.

MEDITATION IS CRITICAL TO WALKING IN THE LIGHT

Meditation, like prayer, is one of those basic ingredients that just helps bring things all together. Virtually everything said about prayer is also true of meditation. Meditation will help you fully manifest love, compassion, empathy, gratitude, and forgiveness. The way meditation helps is like prayer in many respects, but different. Prayer operates more within the mind to help you focus on the things of Christ. Meditation is more of a deeper soul practice to instill and focus you in much the same way. Both are important and the two together help you grow and manifest the things of God better.

Many Christians may be leery of meditation, but as we will see, meditation is perfectly in line with faith and a requirement. Can you walk in the Light without meditation? To some extent yes. Could you walk in the Light without daily prayer or the word? Maybe not very well and eventually you may hit a wall. You're like a car running on fumes or not getting everything it needs to keep running and moving forward. If we want to be truly transformed and produce much fruit, we will want to use every tool we can to follow Christ.

Think of meditation in your walk as warp speed. The starship Enterprise on star trek is always moving fast through space, but when Picard orders the ship to go into warp, it's a zoom! They propel into a flash of light and are gone! I've found that meditation is my warp speed to walk as a Child of the Light. Nothing for me has been as powerful in moving me in the Light. This isn't in any way to denigrate anything else, for, in fact, meditation has helped me to pray better and integrate the word into me.

THE PRACTICE OF CHRISTIAN MEDITATION

Is meditation truly compatible with Christianity? I believe that it's not only compatible but commanded as our opening scripture in Philippians 4:8 says "Finally, brethren, whatever things are true, whatever things are noble, whatever things are just, whatever things are pure, whatever things are lovely, whatever things are of good report, if there is any virtue and if there is anything praiseworthy—meditate on these things." Meditation is simply a time to deeply reflect on things of value. It can also be a time to take things to heart and gain new insights. Meditation is a time to quiet the restless mind and rest in God's presence. Meditation is being aware within a hyper-relaxed state.

Meditating on the things of God can give you understanding,

as it says in Psalms 119:27 "Make me understand the way of Your precepts; So shall I meditate on Your wonderful works. This is the wisdom that can come through meditation. You can hear from God, but also simply gain clarity as you sit in the stillness of your mind and heart. The wonders of God can have so many aspects, you would never run out of things to meditate on. The verse in Philippians covers anything positive, such as love, purity, and goodness. When I think of the wonders of God, I think of beauty. The beauty that He has created as well as the beauty within God Himself. We are part of the beauty of God. The wonderful works include God's blessings and provisions that He gives us.

We can also meditate on the laws of God as it says in Psalms 1:2 "But his delight is in the law of the Lord, And in His law, he [a]meditates day and night." This would include the 612 laws of the Old Testament, but I take the verse much more broadly than that. Any law or principle God has laid down is something that we can meditate on. What does it mean to love one another? What does it mean to love our enemy? What does the golden rule of "Do unto others as you would have them do to you" entail? As you can guess, you have so many directions you could go with meditation.

Meditation in scripture was about going off into the quietness to spend time with God and to become still. Psalms 46:10 "Be still, and know that I am God". Often it is in the stillness that we hear God and feel his presence. It is where we can "know" Him in a more profound way. In Psalms 4:4 it says "Meditate within your heart on your bed, and be still.". Notice it says to meditate within your heart, which is a deep reflection within your being. To truly meditate deeply, you must be still. The verse also gives you a place to meditate, which is your bed, a place of rest. Are you limited to a bed in a strict sense? I don't believe so, but where you meditate should be a comfortable place. I have recently started to lie down during meditation on my bed. Sometimes I still sit comfortably in my easy chair with my eyes closed.

We can meditate on virtually anything that is positive and of God. In Psalm 77:6 the Psalmist speaks of meditating on the Lord's song "I call to remembrance my song in the night; I meditate within my heart, And my spirit [a]makes diligent search.". What is this song? Probably any song of God or simply to focus on a melody within your heart. When I meditate within my heart, it could be on one of the Psalms, many of which were created to be sung.

Meditation was a practice in scripture going way back to even the patriarchs, as it says in Genesis 46:63 "And Isaac went out to meditate in the field in the evening". I sometimes think we mystify meditation and make it totally esoteric. Really, it need not be thought of in that way. It is simply a time to be in close communion with God within our soul. Meditation can be a formal practice, but can also occur informally as well. Many reading this may be informally meditating and not be aware of it. Even listening quietly to a piece of classical music being in total peace for a few minutes can be meditative.

The Apostle Paul encouraged us to examine ourselves to see if we are in the faith in II Corinthians 13:5 "Examine yourselves as to whether you are in the faith. Test yourselves. Do you not know yourselves, that Jesus Christ is in you?" How do you examine yourself without looking deep within your heart and soul, which is to meditate on it? You can not only meditate to see if you are in the faith but if you are walking according to the faith. You can use this time to examine whether you're growing and how you've grown in Him. You can see if Christ is in you and how Christ is working within you as well. When we meditate, we become one with God's Spirit and can tap into His wisdom. We can also tap into the deeper part within ourselves. Romans 2:15 says "who show the work of the law written in their hearts, their conscience also bearing witness, and between themselves their thoughts accusing or else excusing them " In meditation, you can access God's truth that He has placed in your heart. Meditation helps to reduce distractions and allows you to hear the truth more clearly.

Does this mean that all forms of meditation are compatible with Christianity? No, if you're meditating in a way that honors other deities or involves idols, that wouldn't be compatible with Christianity. I would also encourage anyone to avoid mantras to deities or words you have absolutely no idea what they mean. You can do affirmations in your own language for the things of God, such as compassion or love. Just because some forms of meditation may not be compatible with Christianity in no way means all meditation is incompatible with the faith. Just as there are some forms of prayer that are not compatible with the faith as well. No one would ever say prayer is not part of our faith.

In my book "Meditation for Everyone: How to Quickly have a more peaceful, mindful, and fulfilled life", I presented a non-sectarian approach to meditation that was open to anyone, regardless of their faith or no faith at all.[10] I presented basic practices of meditation but in no way presented anything incompatible with Christianity.

What about meditation that tries to "empty your mind"? Some Christians would argue that this type of meditation is not permissible with Christianity because you may open yourself up to hearing from Satan. If one is a believer, though, this is questionable. I would say such forms of meditation are a gray area. It may be ok, but personally, I've never been able to do it the few times I tried many years ago. I don't practice or teach any type of emptying your mind meditation today nor did I in "Meditation for Everyone". I teach a reflective meditation on God and the things of God.

Though I wrote it from a secular perspective, I actually gave a template for meditation built around the Fruits of the Holy Spirit which are love, joy, peace, patience, kindness, goodness, faithfulness, gentleness, and self-control. These principles are part of our faith but are universally embraced by most people as excellent qualities. Within Christian meditation, we can take these qualities in a more overtly Christian way. We also recognize God directly in the process and His Spirit at work in this process. We can also give God the glory specifically. These qualities meditated on can bring greater peace, joy, and fulfillment in life, but when you add a more explicit recognition of our God, you take it to deeper levels.

THE BENEFITS OF MEDITATION

Virtually every benefit that prayer can give you that we covered in the previous chapter is also produced in meditation, but a bit differently. These benefits include manifesting greater love, joy, peace, compassion, gratitude, and empathy. They both work to change your mind and heart, but I think prayer starts and operates primarily on the mind. It will sink down to the heart, but the focal point is a conscious mind. Meditation has a focus more at a heart and soul level. It uses the mind for sure and will eventually change the mind, but the work is more of a heart-centered one. They both overlap with each other but have a somewhat different emphasis. One isn't better than the other and both help you with each other. They can work synergistically to help you more fully walk as a child of the Light. It's interesting that the first greatest commandment was not simply to "Love God", but to love God with everything within you. To love within your entire being. As Luke 10:27 says, "You shall love the Lord your God with all your heart, with all your soul, with all your strength, and with all your mind,". You want to develop a complete picture of your love for God and others in your life. Meditation with prayer helps to put that together for you nicely.

Meditation helps to bring calmness to a person in both mind and body. You slow both mind and body down and just take time to focus on the things of God, such as love and peace.

You turn off the noise that is out there in the world for a short period and can now decompress from the stress in your life. Meditation is one of the best ways to practice relaxation. Meditation helps to eliminate stressful days as well. Beyond just reducing normal day-to-day stress, meditation has been shown to lower depression and has even been used to aid people who suffer from post-traumatic stress disorder (PTSD).[11] I can tell you that I've used meditation to help combat my own issues of depression in the past. I went through a period around 2008 that was especially trying on me.

Meditation helps to improve your concentration and focus, which can be helpful when you're trying to study things like your Bible! It can also help if you're a student or just someone trying to learn new things. Meditation has also been shown to help people who have attention deficit disorder and attention deficit hyperactivity disorder (ADD/ADHD). Meditation helps to improve the grey matter in your brain and can improve intelligence. It literally makes you smarter!

I find that meditation can help me gain clarity on the scriptures both as a matter of a clearer mind in general but also because I'm being still and open to hearing from God to gain additional understanding.

Meditation has been shown to reduce pain and has specifically been used to help treat people who suffer from chronic pain. Everyone wants to think and feel better, but you should specifically want this if you're seeking to walk as a child of the Light. You're more motivated to read your bible, pray, and serve others when you aren't in pain or having brain fog.[12]

It's clear from both a spiritual and mental health perspective that meditation is a wonderful thing. You can and should seek to use meditation to improve both. My book "Meditation for Everyone" focused primarily on the mental health benefits but also supported the spiritual benefits as well. The two go hand in hand. Meditating on being more compassionate is obviously a spiritual quality, but has been found to be of tremendous benefit to mental health. This is true of so many spiritual values, such as forgiveness.

THE KEYS TO MEDITATION

There are three keys to a solid meditation practice which are stillness, mindfulness, and affirmations with gratitude. Someone could take alone any of the three to form a meditation practice, but together, they create a dynamic approach to meditation. The three build on each other and work together to help a person more effectively meditate.

Stillness

Stillness is where you want to still the body and slow the mind down. You seek to be completely still to become more calm and peaceful within. You want to be still both in terms of physical stillness of the body as well as stilling your mind. Stilling the body is the easier part, you stop all movement within the body or at least try to keep movement to a minimum. You can do some adjustments to become fully comfortable, but once you're comfortable, seek to remain as motionless as you can. Stilling the body will help to relax the mind.

A few illustrations may help you picture and capture the idea of stillness. Think of yourself being a caveman within your mind who is frozen in an enormous block of ice. Close your eyes and imagine yourself as that caveman in the block of ice. You've been there for thousands of years, just completely still in the ice. Time passes you by, but you remain unmoved just watching everything go by.

Another illustration is to see yourself in a large body of water, like a lake. The lake is calm and placid. There's only slight motion within that lake. You're floating, just being directed by the lake, you may even begin to feel one with the lake. Close your eyes and only feel the lake, aware of nothing else around you. You feel completely relaxed and at peace in this lake. It's like floating on the lake on a warm summer's day without a care in the world.

A final illustration is to envision yourself within the Light of God. The Light is pure and brings total peace, love, and joy to you. You're totally immersed in this Light and find yourself blending with it. Seeing yourself in this Light can still you and be used as a tool while you meditate on the things of God such as love, compassion, peace. It reinforces your reflections but also further puts you at ease as you meditate.

There are many techniques to become still for meditation or simply to relax at any given moment. One of which is simply to visualize one of the above illustrations, or come up with one of your own. Another is to take 5 to 10 deep breaths through the nose and exhale through the mouth. You breathe in through the nose, hold the breath for approximately 8 seconds. Then you exhale through your mouth. You may also find stillness through sound and music. I love nature sounds which can be actual sounds around you such as birds outside, or you may find recordings such as on YouTube. In terms of music, you can choose gentle meditation music or any instrumental music that you find relaxing, such as classical music. I recommend one piece of meditation music later that you can use.

You can find stillness with a special location such as your favorite easy chair to sit in or a special place outside, maybe a porch swing or hammock. You can create a few affirmations to silently repeat to yourself in your mind such as "I am calm and at peace" or "my mind and body are completely relaxed". You should create some of your own as well. You can create ones from scripture that bring peace to you.

You can use any of the techniques separately, but you may find that combining them will help to still your mind and body the most. Stillness is good for both basic relaxation and as part of a more formal meditation practice. You can do mini-meditations that are anywhere from 1 to 5 minutes during the day using stillness or the other keys to meditation.

Mindfulness

Mindfulness is being aware of your thoughts and the world around you and being completely present in the moment. You are completely in the now. You focus your mind on your thoughts and what is going on around you, but you want to redirect your thoughts and be completely conscious of them. If you're washing the dishes, you may focus your entire attention on the process, noticing each detail such as scrubbing the dish and seeing it become cleaner. If a car goes by and you see it in the window, you stop to notice it and focus on it with your full attention. Think of mindfulness as taking time to stop and smell the flowers in life.

Mindfulness also can be focused not simply on things outside you but your own thoughts themselves. You may stop to focus intently on a thought. With mindfulness of thought, you want to see them and allow them to go by without judgment. This can help as you're meditating trying to focus on love and then you get a thought about a bill you need to pay this week. You notice it, note, and allow it to pass on, quickly redirecting back to love or whatever you were meditating on. Mindfulness is about the acceptance of all things. You accept where you are and what you may be thinking about. You accept yourself in that moment. Passing no judgments and acceptance in that moment are closely connected, like two sides to the same coin.

You can be mindful throughout your day. You probably already are at times, but now you are consciously seeking to do this. In meditation, you can be mindful of how you feel in that moment and possibly why. You can focus on your breathing and heartbeat. You can focus on how relaxed your body is in the chair or lying down. As you can see, mindfulness and stillness go hand-in-hand and work together. To some extent, they overlap. You're still in mind and body but fully aware at the same time. You can be aware of how still you are and how pleasant that feels!

Affirmation with Gratitude

Affirmations are the third component in meditation. Affirmations can help to still you as we have seen but can do much more than that. You can create affirmations to instill beliefs within you and create a more positive view around you. Once you're mindful and still, you can then begin to affirm positive beliefs within yourself such as "I'm a loving and kind person", "I'm God's child", or "I can do all things through Christ which strengthens me". Again, you can create your own affirmations as well. Affirmations can be used with stillness and mindfulness in meditation or can be used anytime to help reprogram your thinking. I do affirmations during my meditation sessions, but also when I go to bed and wake up. You could do them anytime throughout the day. Affirmations in meditation are powerful and affirmations after your prayer time can be a powerful use of them as well. Don't worry about whether you actually believe the affirmations when you first start, chances are, you probably don't. At a conscious or unconscious level, you probably don't completely believe them. As you do affirmations, though, your beliefs at both levels will begin to change. It will most likely be gradual, but every time you will start to walk in the affirmations. I often catch myself repeating an affirmation in my mind as I go about my day. It's so wonderful, your heart feels so good, and you start to really embrace these new beliefs. One such affirmation is about seeing the dignity and beauty in all things and all people. That has been a powerful one for me. I often get waves of love and compassion that just flow over me!

You should affirm what you're grateful for or should be grateful for. Affirm your blessings. I've noticed that as I express what I'm grateful for in affirmations, I begin to feel more grateful within my heart. When you affirm gratitude like this, it can become a deep prayer within you of gratitude for God, recognizing that all blessings ultimately come from Him. Affirm blessings both past, present, and future. You want to affirm the good things God has done for you and what He is doing for you. You also want to affirm that you trust Him to continue blessing and caring for you in the future.

THE CONNECTION BETWEEN PRAYER AND MEDITATION

Prayer and meditation have a strong connection with each other and make each other more powerful when used together.

Two Sides To The Same Coin

Meditation and prayer, to a great extent, are two sides to the same coin. In prayer, you are speaking to God with your mind and sometimes mouth. Meditation is taking time to hear the still small voice of God within you as well as capture His truth within your soul, listening to the deeper part of yourself. Meditation is the flip side of the coin where you are listening in many cases for God rather than speaking directly to Him. Meditation is where you are in a highly relaxed state, both mind and body, yet you're fully aware at the same time.

Is meditation the same as sleep? Because meditation can put you in such a deeply relaxed state, many may be tempted to think of sleep and meditation in the same way. When you sleep, though, you are not generally aware of what you're doing or what is going on around you. Meditation, though extremely calming, is an active practice within your being. I can attest, I love to meditate in the afternoon and have had an afternoon nap before. They are radically different, both in what you experience during the nap and what you experience during meditation. The experience afterward tends to be radically different. After a nap, you generally tend to feel groggy and it takes a while to fully awake. Meditation, when done properly, doesn't tend to give you that groggy feeling. Meditation for me actually makes me feel more rested and awake than a nap. Both can positively change your mood to a better one, but meditation surpasses what you can get from a nap. Meditation can give you a super energetic feeling at times, even to the point of euphoria. I don't always get that euphoric feeling, but I can have it at times both during and after meditation. When my mind and body are at peace during meditation and I'm aware, it can feel so great that I call that state the "tranquility zone". Both sleep and meditation do alter the level of consciousness your brain is operating in from a normal awake state.

Meditation and Contemplative Prayer

I put together a short video that was posted on Facebook and YouTube, where I discuss the aspects of stillness in meditation.[13] One person told me she had never meditated, but that my teaching on meditation was similar to contemplative prayer, which she practiced. I have not studied contemplative prayer extensively. It didn't surprise me. In contemplative prayer, you seek to become still and focus your attention on a word or concept focused toward God. It's sometimes called the "gaze of faith". This involves a deep focus within your heart and soul toward God. Many Christian groups and denominations practice contemplative prayer. You can go back to the early church, such as the desert fathers, to find both meditation and deep prayer becoming a practice. Both the Eastern and Western churches promote vocal prayer, meditation, and contemplative prayer, with the 3 being connected and representing different levels of communion with God.[14]

I can see the similarity in that I place a focus within myself during my meditation. For example, my focus might be love or compassion. I would say that the meditation practice that I teach is probably less rigid than contemplative prayer because you can shift focus within meditation from different concepts. You also use affirmations, visualizations, a focus on breath or heartbeat, or simply be still in His presence. I think this is true for some schools of meditation, which also teach a very rigid approach to the practice. Some will focus exclusively on repeating one word (mantras) or just on breath. I teach to mix it up a bit during a session. For one, it is less boring and easier to keep focused than a one hat trick. Two, it keeps you from simply falling asleep during your meditation. If I was to repeat the same word over and over such as love, and that's all I did, I would probably fall asleep after 30 minutes. Many of you reading this would as well.

Since meditation, like contemplative prayer, can be focused on God and concepts connected to God, we can see it as a type of prayer itself. If you affirm good things in your life and hold a grateful feeling within your heart, that can be a deep-seated prayer within your heart too deep for the conscious mind or the mouth to speak. It's not a replacement for typical prayer by any means, but something that works with your regular prayers to communicate with God and be in His presence.

In terms of altering your brain, meditation and deep forms of prayer, such as contemplative prayer, can alter how your brain works. It calms your mind, which can last for a significant time after meditation. Scientific studies have noted these changes.[15] Another experience that can alter your brain waves in a similar way to contemplative prayer and meditation is people who have had near-death experiences, which is another topic of interest to me and for which I wrote a book. Why does this change occur? Well, the brain is slowed down in processing, that's what we see in scientific studies. It's important to note that with meditation, deep prayer, and the near-death experience, it in no way impairs your mental faculties but helps you more effectively and calmly process information. I believe there is another factor. All three experiences put the person in a deeply spiritual state and connect the person to God in a profound way. Obviously, the NDE is the most profound connection with the spiritual realm, more profound than meditation or contemplative prayer, but many NDEers take up meditation after their near-death experience to try to recreate the experience they had with the Light of God. Most would say it's not as profound, but it does get them closer to that state than anything else short of dying again. The one person I mentioned who does contemplative prayer actually had 4 NDEs and uses that practice to more deeply connect with God.

MEDITATION AND THE WORD

We have looked at several verses on meditating on the law of God as well as meditating on things that are good and noble which come from scripture. Should we actually meditate on scripture itself and are all scriptures potentially advantageous to meditate on. The answer is yes, especially portions that point you to something positive in your life. Meditation has a way of planting the seeds of scripture deep in your heart. Take what you may have read and meditate on it. You may have memorized scripture in the past or be memorizing scriptures now. What you have memorized can be a great source of meditation. Both in terms of reciting the verse and putting it within your being, but to also gain understanding and clarity. God may more fully reveal things in those verses you had not considered before meditating on it. Maybe you've memorized them but never stopped to reflect on what it is you've memorized or only looked at it on a surface level. You may have said "oh, that's a good verse" quickly moving on.

Psalms 49:3 says "My mouth shall speak wisdom, And the meditation of my heart shall give understanding." What words in his mouth are likely to bring wisdom? These would be the words or teachings from God for sure. Where can we get these teachings from God readily? The scriptures, of course! Notice the second part of the verse says that the meditation of the heart will bring understanding. When we meditate, we gain a deeper understanding of the wisdom of scripture if we focus on it. You understand it not only at a surface level but deep within your soul and when that happens, you can more fully walk it out. Both the Eastern and Western churches practiced deep meditation of the scriptures in the monasteries going back several centuries. You don't have to be in a monastery to benefit from meditating on the word. You can do it where you are. This is critical to transforming the world for Christ, moving these powerful practices out of just the monasteries and into the homes of everyday people.

In Psalms 119:11 it says, "Your word I have hidden in my heart, That I might not sin against You." How do you hide these words in your heart or plant them? By memorization, sure, but meditation will plant what is memorized more deeply. In fact, just 4 verses later in verse 15 the writer says, "I will meditate on Your precepts, And [b]contemplate Your ways." By meditating on scripture, you will keep yourself from sinning. Sin is anything contrary to His law, which is rooted in love. So sin is anything contrary to love. Sin is missing the mark of love. To walk in love and the qualities of love, you should meditate on the things of scripture.

LET IT GO WITH MEDITATION

One thing you will do with meditation is to let go of everything that is going on in your life during your session, however long that is. What does this mean? Remember in prayer, we discussed how you unburden yourself by casting all your concerns onto God? In a sense, it's like that, but in another sense, it's completely the opposite. You will unburden yourself of the cares, but not by focusing on them and talking about them directly with God. With meditation, you unburden by leaving the cares of this world at the door and go into a completely different frame of mind. You want to take in a positive focus such as we have been discussing, which can include scriptures, the Fruits of the Spirit, and other uplifting things. You use your affirmations, gratitude, visualization, stilling, and mindfulness altogether. I consciously tell myself sometimes that I'm leaving all this world at the door with all its distractions to go to a different space. This includes not only the stresses of this world and the mundane things. It should even include the exciting things as well. Why is that? Because they can distract you and keep you from going more deeply within your meditation.

With a different application of letting go of this world that meditation has from prayer, is one better than the other? No! In fact, you need to have both to cope with stress and spiritually let go. They both provide a cathartic experience, but from a different angle. Sometimes you need to take your mind off things and go somewhere else, and sometimes you need to talk it out.

What are some common things you will specifically need to let go during your meditation? You want to release all judgments for this time. This is an aspect of mindfulness, as we saw. This person is doing this wrong or that wrong, or I'm doing this or that wrong. Just let all that go for this short time. Let all prejudices go as well. Meditation will help to release prejudice in your life, but choose to let them go specifically and see how much faster they will go!

Let all anger and bitterness go. Hopefully, you will let them go permanently, but choose for this time to shelf them. What's funny, you may forget them on the shelf and just leave them there. Even if you remember them later, you may decide to just keep them there or just completely toss them in the mental trash can completely. Meditation has a way of releasing anger and bitterness that you may be holding on to and can help to reduce the chances or impact of you becoming angry or bitter in the future.

You will want to let go of any low self-esteem, you're not going to be thinking trash about yourself during meditation, or trash about anyone else. If you are going into your meditation feeling down on yourself, you can make it a point to affirm who you are in Christ and what He is building in you. You might affirm "I'm a winner in Christ", "God is doing a wonderful new work in me", "I can succeed in Him". You can come up with more, and we will give more as this book unfolds.

MAKING MEDITATION A PRIORITY

Many people will say that they don't have the time to meditate, it's like anything else, you have to make time; It has to become a priority in your life. Consistency is a key to meditation. You will never realize the full benefits of meditation doing it sporadically, just as you will not with occasional prayer. Yes, you can meditate from time to time and get short-term benefits such as relaxation, but you will never get the long-term benefits of consistent meditation. You will not even get the same benefits in the short term because meditation is a skill developed over time. Commit today to start a regular meditation practice.

I recommend building up to at least a 30-minute meditation a day. I personally meditate about 45 minutes a day on average. This may sound like a lot, but to get the full benefits of meditation, you need at least 30 minutes. I speak from personal experience, you can get benefits from as little as 5 to 10 minutes a day as some suggest, but if you take it to 30, it's a real game-changer! If you want to walk as a child in the Light, I recommend you take full advantage of meditation by giving yourself enough time.

I do realize that going from no meditation and immediately starting with a 30-minute practice may be difficult at first, so I suggest working up to it. You can start with 5 minutes to meditate at first. A good way to slowly build up and acclimate to meditating for longer durations is to meditate for 5 minutes the first day and add a minute each day to your session. In less than a month, you will be meditating for 30 minutes! Of course, if you want or can meditate longer to start, go for it! If you can do 10 or 15 to start, that's great. Another tactic to start meditation is to do what I call mini-meditations at different points throughout the day. These can be as short as 1 to 3 minutes. With mini-meditations, I'm not as strict on the rules. You might use music or not, you might sit in a regular chair at the table. You might find time to squeeze in a mini-meditation while you're waiting for a bus or doing laundry. Any downtime presents the possibility to do a mini-meditation.

With mini-meditations, you could take what you learn with stillness and apply those to your sessions. A piece of music, visualization, a few calming affirmations, or a special location. These are the basic tools to take into a longer, more formal meditation as well.

With a regular meditation practice, you will want to find a time and place that works for you. I personally love afternoon meditations. I find them to be the most beneficial. I receive greater relaxation and energy than at any other time when I meditate. If this doesn't work for you, consider a morning or evening meditation. You might need to experiment with times until you find what works best for you. I've had to find time to meditate in different situations. When my son was young, and I was taking care of him, I meditated during nap times. When He started school, I did it before He got home. When I worked one job, I would use my lunch break to do my meditation and then just scarf down my lunch.

You will also need a place that is relatively quiet. One thing that can help if you can't find a completely quiet place is noise-canceling headphones. You listen to meditation music with your headphones on. You may like the headphones even if the room is quiet, but I personally like the music to play over a speaker, that's a matter of personal preference. Find a comfortable place to meditate where you're not likely to be disturbed. Where might this place be for you? Maybe a home office? An easy chair in the living room? Possibly your bedroom on the bed might work. Just make sure that if you're constantly falling asleep that you find another location. You might even find meditating in your regular chair to be a comfortable place to meditate. You can meditate outside but do take weather into consideration. The place might work in the summer but maybe not in the winter where you live. You can pick a seasonal place to meditate, but have one in mind for the rest of the year.

STARTING A MEDITATION PRACTICE

Once you find a place and time to meditate and are ready to start, go to that place. Close your eyes and take in 5 to 10 deep breaths to start. Remember, you breathe through your nose, hold for approximately 8 seconds. Then exhale through your mouth. Once you complete these deep breaths, you may breathe more normally through your nose. After a few minutes, your breathing should become calm and shallow. Throughout your meditation, you can come back to your breath to focus on it. Breath is a good focal point to refocus you during your meditation. It can both still you and help you be more mindful. I often come back to my breath during a meditation several times in a session. Some types of meditation exclusively have you focus on the breath for meditation. I don't think this is necessary and believe you can focus on other things, but breath is always generally a good option. Breath is a tool, though, in your meditation toolkit for sure. Breath might be like your screwdriver.

Another way to bring your focus back while meditating is to focus on your heartbeat. If you find your mind getting caught with distractions, you can direct your attention to notice your heart beating. I will occasionally use this technique as an alternative to noticing my breath.

When you're first starting out to meditate, you can do a head-to-toe meditation where you start at your head and focus your attention on it. Take a deep breath and release. See your head relax. Then you work your way down your body till you get to your toes. I have a video called "Body Scan Meditation Guided Meditation to introduce you to mindfulness meditation."[16] That is a head-to-toe meditation. You can also use this meditation when you're distracted or just can't get into meditation. It takes about 5 to 10 minutes. You can go on from there to meditate on other things after that. I only use body meditation now when I'm distracted. This probably will not be something you do in most meditations once you get used to the practice.

I use a template for meditation centered on the Fruits of the Holy Spirit. You can start with the nine fruits of love, joy, peace, patience, kindness, goodness, faithfulness, gentleness, and self-control. You can take one fruit for each session or a few fruits to meditate on. Sometimes I will even meditate on all of them during a session. It depends on how in-depth or focused you wish to be in that session. You can create affirmations about them that incorporate what you're grateful for and what you want to affirm about yourself. You can visualize each fruit. You can create symbols in your mind to help you focus on the qualities. Maybe you visualize peace as a peach tree. You might see everything about that tree within your mind. You may taste it. Let this become a picture of peace within you, sweet and delicious. Someone might also picture peace as a pool of warm water, that puts you in a peaceful state, maybe like a Jacuzzi. You can use visualization to help you meditate. You may focus on what the fruits mean, both personally and generally. What does love mean to you? Who do you love? Who loves you? Allow yourself to feel the love of God in your meditation.

Something I highly recommend for meditation is listening to good meditation music. You can find thousands of choices on YouTube for free. The music will help to better focus your mind and relax you. The music should be instrumental and peaceful sounding. It should not be overwhelming or too fast in its beat. Any type of ambient or meditation music will usually work well. You may need to experiment. You should also change it up from time to time. Listening to the same piece of music all the time can grow stale. One piece I would suggest starting out with is called "Inner Peace Sleep Meditation Music, Music for Deep Sleep, Music for Meditation, Concentration Music"[17] which can be found on YouTube. It's a tranquil piece of music.

You really want to eventually get to at least 30 minutes of meditation a day, which may seem like a lot but it's what you need to really get the full benefits out of meditation. If you want to reach the tranquility zone in meditation, you will have to give yourself enough time, and you want to stay in this zone for a while, not abruptly ending your meditation session. If you need to start with 5 minutes a day and work up, that's fine, but have your goal to be ultimately 30 minutes. Nothing has transformed my walk in the Light like meditation. This time is a deep communion with God and a connection with your own soul. The time spent meditating is sacred and should be viewed as such. To fully walk in everything else taught in this book, you need daily meditation in your life.

MY OWN JOURNEY WITH MEDITATION

I first started meditating in 2005, primarily to experience more peace and have a tool for relaxation. It was great for unwinding. I found that whenever I did meditate; I did feel more peaceful and relaxed. I could decompress from a day doing it. This is probably why most people start to meditate at first. I wasn't consistent when I first started meditating. Sometimes my meditations were sporadic. I meditated for about 20 minutes when I did meditate until several years later when I increased it to about 30 minutes. Using meditation as a nice pick-me-up was great until around 2008 when I began to suffer from depression in my life. I was having financial issues, which led to me losing my house. I was also feeling lonely wanting someone; I was 36 at the time. God brought a woman into my life that would eventually become my wife, which was great. I did notice that even the sporadic meditations of 20 minutes would give some relief from the depression, but it was temporary. During the meditation and a few hours after, I would feel better. This was much like aspirin for a headache, but now I was having chronic headaches. This did propel me to gradually become more serious about my meditation. I was still inconsistent but was starting to be less sporadic in my meditations because I realized they helped.

It wasn't until 2010 that I was committed to meditation on a daily basis. The habit of faithfully meditating each day still was not overnight. I tend to procrastinate badly on virtually everything, and meditation back then was no different. It was one of those things that the more I meditated, the more benefit I received, which inspired me to be more consistent. I noticed that meditation could be more than just a quick momentary aspirin fix, but could improve your overall mental health. You could reduce depression from occurring in the first place while experiencing other benefits in the process.

Meditation has been a way for me to gain clarity within my soul. I understand myself much better. I also noticed that through meditation while being quiet, I could hear the still, small voice of God, who gave me more understanding and peace. I noticed over the years that meditation helped me to be less angry and more forgiving, to let things go easier. To be more gentle and less reactive with people.

Meditation has been a godsend for me in virtually every area of my life, which includes spiritually, emotionally, and physically. The thing with meditation is that you can experience benefits from day one as I did just starting out 16 years ago, but over time and as you gain consistency, you will gain further benefits. I'm still finding additional benefits of meditation and growing in the benefits it's already given me today.

I can say, if you want to walk as a child of the Light, to be more loving, compassionate, peaceful, kind, patient, and apply everything else in scripture that you read about, you SHOULD start practicing meditation. It's been the most effective tool in my arsenal and helps me apply all the other tools in the box more effectively. Meditation is my time to simply sit in the presence of God and plant seeds within my soul. It's a time to turn the world off with all its distractions and focus on all things good from

God. It's a time to energize myself to go live the life I want to live in Christ and the life I know God wants me to live.

Application

1. Take time right now to stop and do a mini-meditation using some or all the tools given to you in this chapter, which includes breathing, finding an excellent location, music, visualization of something calming, and affirmations. I recommend you take 5 breaths and just do one or two affirmations to start. This can include an affirmation of "I am calm and at peace". Remember, a mini-meditation can be as short as 1 to 3 minutes, but if you're feeling great and want to spend more time, go for it! Mini-meditations are a great way to help prepare you for longer meditations, and you can use them throughout the day to become more meditative in day-to-day living.

2. Try to think of a time and location you can do your longer meditations each day. You want a set time, such as morning, afternoon, or night. If you can come up with an exact time, such as 1:00 PM or 8:00 AM, that's even better. Commit to consistent meditation each day. You should do some experimenting at first to find which time and location works best for you.

3. Once you have a time and location, start meditating each day! You can start with the music piece I suggested, which is "Inner Peace Sleep Meditation Music, Music for Deep Sleep, Music for Meditation, Concentration Music" on YouTube. Remember to do 10 deep breaths to start. Try to come up with at least 5 affirmations you can do during your meditation.

4. THE WORD

"So shall My word be that goes forth from My mouth; It shall not return to Me void, But it shall accomplish what I please, And it shall prosper in the thing for which I sent it." (Isaiah 55:11)

THE WORD WILL ACCOMPLISH GREATNESS IN YOU

In Isaiah 55:11, we read that "So shall My word be that goes forth from My mouth; It shall not return to Me void, But it shall accomplish what I please, And it shall prosper in the thing for which I sent it." If you take in and apply the word, it will not come back empty to you. It will accomplish great things in your life. It will prosper you in all things that it is intended to prosper you in. What does this mean? Is it talking about prosperity in a financial sense, which is a common teaching in some circles? No, prosperity is spiritual prosperity. Any good thing, spiritually, will be manifest in you. Everything we spoke of in chapter one, such as walking in the kingdom which is love, peace, and righteousness, is going to be established in you. You may benefit from certain spiritual qualities, such as greater peace and joy in your mental or physical health as well. But they are an outgrowth of the spiritual prosperity being developed in you.

Something closely connected to prosperity is having the ability to have what we want to be done for us. In the world, we often see success as getting what you want in life. The scriptures actually teach that if you abide in the word, you can have all things. John 15:7 "If you abide in Me, and My words abide in you, you[a] will ask what you desire, and it shall be done for you.". This is where many prosperity teachers go crazy. Oh, does this mean I get the Mercedes, mansion, and private jet? Some unfortunately teach things like this. When you follow God, He starts to change your desires. As it says in Philippians 2:13, it says, "For God is working in you, giving you the desire and the power to do what pleases Him." So as you abide in his word and the Spirit works within your heart, your desires change from one of selfishness and materialism to that of love, kindness, compassion, and peace. This is the "catch" if you want God to give you the desires of your heart. He may still give you certain material things, though you're not guaranteed them. If your heart is in God, you will seek to use those things to further walking in the Light.

THE WORD IS THE STANDARD

The scriptures are integral to living out the Christian life. It's the foundation of our spiritual house God is building within us. As II Timothy 2:16, 17 says, "All Scripture is given by inspiration of God, and is profitable for doctrine, for reproof, for correction, for [c]instruction in righteousness, that the man of God may be complete, thoroughly equipped for every good work." Notice first, that God inspires the scriptures, which literally means God-breathed in Greek. We can find the fingerprint of God throughout the scriptures. Both the internal and external consistency of the Bible attests to this as well. The Bible has stood the test of time and is one of the most reliable works within the ancient world. Many fulfilled prophecies help to verify that it has a divine imprint. It has been a constant source of inspiration to believers throughout the centuries.

God gave the scriptures for doctrine. Remember that the word doctrine simply means teaching. This includes teachings about the nature of God and Christ and the teaching of who we are and how we should live. God has written the truth on our hearts, which is why people universally condemn things like murder and stealing, but the word helps to solidify the truth already in our hearts and expand upon that truth. It helps to clarify such truth as well. We know from scripture not only the negative laws such as not to kill but the positive ones such as treating others with love and kindness.

The scriptures can give reproof when we go into error. This may come from others sharing it with us, or we may read it for ourselves. Often it's not so much that we don't know the truth, though that can happen. More often, we need to be reminded of the truth. We need to be reminded to show love, kindness, compassion, and forgiveness. We may be angry toward someone and holding, bitterness and then read a passage about the importance of forgiving our neighbors. This may be all we need to change direction back toward the Light.

The Bible instructs us in righteousness so that they may thoroughly equip us to walk in the Light. I think this is especially true as you read through the gospels and teachings of Christ. We think we are doing well when we don't harm others, but Christ gave the command to treat others as we would want them to treat us. We are actively implored to love our neighbors, even our enemies.

The word illuminates the path that we should go for ourselves. Psalms 119:105 says, "Your word is a lamp to my feet And a light to my path." The word is pictured as a lamp that lights the way that we should go. We know that Christ through the Spirit also guides us into the Light by giving us wisdom and power. (I Corinthians 12:7-11). The Spirit often uses the word directly to guide us on our spiritual journey. We have both the testimony of the Spirit and the Word. The testimony of at least 2 witnesses establishes everything (Deuteronomy 19:15). I think this is why I love meditation so much. I can meditate on the word and allow the Spirit to guide me in it. Meditation allows the word and Spirit to work within my heart, mind, and soul.

THE WORD WILL KEEP YOU FROM SIN

The scriptures can actually help to keep you from sinning. As it says in Psalms 119:11, "Your word I have hidden in my heart, That I might not sin against You." How does the word keep us from sin? It keeps us from sin in many ways. For one, it puts our focus on the things of God. This helps to reduce the temptations of the world, as well as the distractions of the world. Not all things are sin, but even some things that aren't sinful in and of themselves can be a distraction to walking as a Child of the Light. The scriptures help to put your gaze directly on the things of God.

A few verses earlier in vs 9, the Psalmist says, "How can a young man keep his way pure? By guarding it according to your word" (ESV) What is purity referring to in this passage? Obviously, it is referring to being sexually pure, which is important as a child of the Light. Promiscuous sex can take us down a path that leads to heartache and selfishness. It can completely distract us from the path of God like virtually nothing else. Paul said that it's the only sin that was against the body itself. (I Corinthians 6:18) Sex is one of the easiest things to become addicted to, and addiction, whether it be sex, drugs, or alcohol, makes it impossible to fully walk in the Kingdom of God. Being ensnared in such sin is like trying to swim with heavyweights tied around our legs.

Does purity in this verse have a broader context as well though? I believe it does. To be pure in all things is to walk in love. If your mind, heart, and actions are pure, they must walk in accordance with love. As you read the word, the most important doctrine is to love. As you read the word, your love for all things pure will grow and you will distance yourself from all things not pure or loving. Going back to sexual purity for a minute. When you engage in sexual activity that is selfish and, let's be honest, we know it's really about what we want. Are you acting in love? Are you showing pure love for the other person? Your actions are not in line with perfect love, is it? In I Corinthians 13:5 it says that love "does not seek its own". Seek to do all things from a pure heart of love, putting others first, and you will keep your ways pure. Staying in the scriptures can help you do this.

Besides love, one of the other fruits of the Spirit is faithfulness. This bears on sex, but really just about anything. When you are faithful to another person, you are loyal to them and committed. You care for that other person and place their needs above your own.

The word is one of the key instruments that help us in sanctification. Sanctification is perfecting our lives. Where we live Godly and away from sin. Remember the second step that happens when you are born of the Spirit? The power of sin lessens more and more as you follow Christ. As we are sanctified, the power of sin grows weaker and weaker. John 17:17 says, "Sanctify[i] them by Your truth. Your word is truth." We see in this verse that the word is truth, and it's this truth that will help to sanctify us. When you immerse yourself in truth, you help to purify and cleanse your soul from the filth of this world. You also take on the nature of Christ. Exposure to the word in all forms is a beautiful thing, whether it's reading, listening, memorizing, or meditating on it. You want to be a doer of the word as it says in James 1:22, "But be doers of the word, and not hearers only, deceiving yourselves." You want to pray and meditate on the word to make it a reality in your life. If you are born of the Spirit, it will become your heart's desire to follow the word. I believe that is what it's referencing when it mentions being deceived. If you can read the word and not have any desire to live it, you may need to pray to be born of the Spirit first.

The word is an active weapon in our struggle to remain pure and be cleansed from the power of sin. In Ephesians 6:17, it says, "And take the helmet of salvation, and the sword of the Spirit, which is the word of God; " The word is the only part of the soldier's uniform that is described as a weapon that a believer has. The word functions both as a defense to distractions of the world and realms of darkness but is an offensive weapon to break the strongholds that those things have in your life. To use this weapon, though, it says to first put on the helmet of salvation. You have to be born of his Spirit to reap the full power of the word.

THE WORD WILL REFRESH YOU

The scriptures can reinvigorate your soul and give you hope. It can pick you up when you're down and revive you. As Psalms 19:7 says, "The law of the Lord is perfect, refreshing the soul. The statutes of the Lord are trustworthy, making wise the simple." (NIV) This passage specifically references the law of the Lord but applies to the entire Bible. What does refresh really mean? It means to revive your energy and vitality. In some translations, they use the word revive. If you're running low, maybe you need to be replenished by scripture. The scriptures can revive us because it is true, or trustworthy. It's a foundation you can rely on in difficult times.

When it says "making wise the simple", it's referring to giving us the wisdom that we need so that we can move from a simple state to a wise one. If you want to grow in wisdom, you need to be in the scriptures and have the scriptures be in you.

Think of the scriptures like a giant glass of cold water on a hot summer's day. How refreshing is it when you're thirsty and drink a glass of cold water? You feel so good. The water not only makes you feel better but is actually helping your body. Drinking enough water can help keep you from dehydration and restore you if you do become dehydrated. The same is true with the scriptures. It can keep us from spiritual dehydration. Many of us today are completely drained spiritually, we are so dehydrated spiritually that we've lost all joy. Refresh yourself in His word daily.

What do we also know about water? It gives life. Without it, we would die within a matter of a few days. Water brings oxygen to our cells to give us life. The scriptures are the same way. It brings life and will keep us from dying spiritually. As Jesus said in John 8:51, "Most assuredly, I say to you, if anyone keeps My word he shall never see death.". Maybe you aren't dead spiritually, but are you running on fumes today?

Jesus compared the scriptures to food in Matthew 4:4 when He said to Satan during his temptation, "It is written, 'Man shall not live by bread alone, but by every word that proceeds from the mouth of God.' "The word is like water on a hot day but is also like food to our body which nourishes it. Scripture can nourish your spiritual body. It will give you everything you need to walk in truth. The scriptures are like a smorgasbord of foods to choose from and consume. We've got your superfoods, your blueberries, and spinach of the word. You've got your proteins like the meat of the word. You've got your tasty stuff like spiritual pizza, but which can also contain many nutrients at the same time. The key is to have a balance of many different things within scripture and seek to take from all of scripture.

It's a matter of consuming it and allowing the word to work itself within your spiritual being. You have to really take it in, not just passively read it, but take it to heart by learning and studying it. Make it a part of you by praying and meditating on it. Apply what you read and walk it out. To be a child of the Light, you have to have the word within you.

There are so many wonderful promises in the Bible, but how will we know what they are unless you are in the word? Reading the word will show you what they are and by being in the word regularly, it will constantly remind you of these promises. Many of us may know the promises, but like most things, we need to be reminded of them regularly.

THE WORD GIVES PROMISE

God has promised to bless those that are in His word. Jesus said in Luke 11:28, "blessed are those who hear the word of God and keep it!" What is a blessing? In scripture, this is walking in God's favor. You are being cared for by God. God is always showering reward on you, both here and in the life to come. We can receive wonderful gifts as we walk in the word. What are these excellent gifts that we are blessed with? They're the gifts we have been talking about throughout this book, namely joy, peace, love, kindness, and compassion. God immerses us in these gifts, but even more so as we are in the world. We also are more aware of these gifts. So much of the time, not that God is not blessing us, it's just that we fail to perceive it in our life. As you read the word, you also can feel the peace, love, and joy more intensely. Your sensitivity is heightened. We spoke of prayer and meditation being beneficial earlier. You want to have good things to focus on during prayer and meditation, and the focal point should be the word. Yes, meditate on things like love, joy, peace, and kindness, but where are these values taught to you? Where are they reinforced for you? It's in the word.

Notice in the verse, it's both in hearing the word and keeping the word that is important. We start by taking in the word through reading and listening to it. Sometimes listening to the word can be as powerful as reading it. One may want to consider listening to the word being read at times. You may be tired or on the go, which can make listening to the word a better option at the moment. You may also sometimes pick up on something as you hear it being read that you might have missed reading through it yourself. Reading the word is wonderful too though, so it's not really that one modality is better than the other. You can actually combine both by reading first and then listening to it be read, or by reading along as they read the word. You have so many options to listen to the Bible being read. Several complete versions of scripture on YouTube are completely free.

The second part of the verse is to keep the word. You don't simply want to read or listen to the word, but you want to apply it to your life. We must be doers of the word. (James 1:22-25). Seek to apply what you read. If it says to serve others, then seek to serve others. If it says to forgive those that hurt you, forgive them. Meditate on what the word teaches and pray that God will give you the heart's desire to apply what you read in scripture.

In Psalms 18:30 it says, "As for God, His way is perfect; The word of the Lord is [h]proven; He is a shield to all who trust in Him." The word is proven and a shield. There is both protection in the word and provision. God will preserve your heart and mind as you read and apply the word. Remember, the word can keep you from sin, and also help you turn from sin. It will shelter you from the temptations of this life. God will provide for your needs, and you will know it more fully as you are in his word. As you read the word, you will begin to trust God more fully. To walk as a child of the Light, you want to have the blessings and provision of God. You wanted to be guarded against going astray. You want to trust in God fully with all your heart and mind.

THE WORD GIVES HOPE

The scriptures is one of the principal sources of hope for a believer. Romans 15:4 says, "For whatever things were written before were written for our learning, that we through the [c]patience and comfort of the Scriptures might have hope." We can derive peace and comfort from the scriptures as we read them and meditate on them. We also know as we read the scriptures that God will grow the seeds of love, kindness, and goodness within us. God will stay close to us, which we will be reminded of continuously in scripture. We know that God and Jesus will stay closer to us than a brother. (Proverbs 18:24) I love the footprints poem where Jesus is walking through life with us, and occasionally carrying us when life becomes too difficult to handle. When you want to know that Jesus has got your hand, or even carrying you, stay in His word.

Sometimes life can become stressful and one of the best ways to combat stress and keep your hope is by being in the word. The word will get you through those difficult times. The scriptures can also help with depression. We all go through times of sorrow, which can lead to depression. We have a source of hope in those times, which is the scriptures. The scriptures can also help to prevent or reduce the times we find ourselves in such emotional states

Jesus had promised to give us life, and that more abundantly. (John 10:10) We can walk in this abundant life partly by taking the word into our hearts and minds. It vastly improves the quality of life that I live as I take time to be in the scriptures.

The scriptures can give us hope by helping to lay a firm foundation for our spiritual lives. As Mathew 7:24 says, "Therefore whoever hears these sayings of Mine, and does them, I will liken him to a wise man who built his house on the rock: " When you lack such a foundation the ground underneath you is like shifting sand which can easily be washed away through trials and tribulations. The Bible is like a foundation of our spiritual house. You can have a well-built home but lack a good foundation. I believe God can speak to us in a variety of ways, but the Bible is foundational in how He speaks to us. It's a foundation that we should not neglect when we want to hear from Him. Often, the Spirit will minister to our hearts, but He tends to draw from scripture or at least things that are taught in scripture. The scripture can confirm what the Spirit may be saying to you in your heart as well. To walk in the Light, we need to hear both the word and Spirit speaking to us and allow them to work together.

The scriptures also help to reinforce the heavenly hope that we have in Christ, as Colossians 3:2-4 says, "Set your mind on things above, not on things on the earth. For you died, and your life is hidden with Christ in God. When Christ who is our life appears, then you also will appear with Him in glory." One way to help combat stress and depression is to also know that we have a hope of life beyond this world, and a life to come that is far better than the earthly life. This world is not all there is, and as we spend time in scripture, this truth can become more real to us. I love what Paul said in Philippians 1:21 "For to me, to live is Christ, and to die is gain. "While we are in this world, we live for Christ. When we pass away, we will have a better life, one that is free of sorrow and pain.

The scriptures will give us hope by guiding us in all truth. As Jesus said in John 8:31, 32 says, "Then Jesus said to those Jews who believed Him, "If you abide in My word, you are My disciples indeed. And you shall know the truth, and the truth shall make you free". The scriptures are true, and we can walk in this truth as we take in the word. Notice too, as we walk in greater truth, we also become free. Truth is liberating! If you want to know the truth and be free, you need to have the word in you. The world seeks after truth but has a million voices going in a million directions. How can we find truth? By his word.

THE WORD GIVES CLARITY

When one thinks of having clarity, you think of a light bulb going off in your head. We need to have things illuminated in order for us to see things clearly. Just like when you enter a dark room and can't see anything, then you turn the light on and everything in the room is now visible to you. You want to see clearly in a spiritual context as well. The word shines that light so we can better see and understand spiritual truth. As Psalms 119:130 says, "The entrance of Your words gives light; It gives understanding to the simple." The word gives light as we go through life and enter new phases of our life. Notice that even if we are not too advanced in our understanding, the word can begin to expand our grasp of things. Often the word doesn't give a specific answer to every question we have, though sometimes it might. What the word does in most cases is give basic spiritual truths that we can then apply to various issues in our life. The Spirit will take the word in our hearts and give us more specific directions on how to apply scripture to a particular situation. This can come in day-to-day living, but can also come during meditation. In meditation, you may ask the Spirit to guide you, and if you are in the word or know it well, you may find that the answers are following scriptural principles. Certainly, they should never violate them. You may not always be aware of the principle at first and may discover it later if you have not come across it in your studies of scripture.

The scriptures give light that will give us a new mindset, one that is centered in love, compassion, and goodness. The word may also help to renew our minds. Remember with prayer, you need a constant refreshing in your life. The word helps to refresh or renew your mind daily. As it says in Romans 12:2 "And do not be conformed to this world, but be transformed by the renewing of your mind, that you may prove what is that good and acceptable and perfect will of God." We don't just read the scriptures once and are done with it. We read them daily, on a regular basis. We need our minds renewed continuously because this world presents an array of distractions that can take us away from the things of God. It's easy even as a believer to slip into thought patterns that are selfish, lustful, prideful, fearful, etc. The word can help to diminish the distractions and keep our focus on track. As we said earlier, you may have read a passage 20 years ago and then read it today and gain things from the passage that you didn't see back then. Maybe you have spiritually matured and are able to now see the truth on a deeper level. Maybe you didn't need what the Spirit is showing you now in it 20 years ago.

The word gives you wisdom as you read and study it. Colossians 3:16 says "Let the word of Christ dwell in you richly in all wisdom, teaching and admonishing one another in psalms and hymns and spiritual songs, singing with grace in your hearts to the Lord." Wisdom is both the knowledge of what spiritual truth is, but more importantly, the ability to apply it in your life and the lives of others. Knowledge by itself can puff a person up (I Corinthians 8:1), so the ability to apply it is critical. The wisdom is not only for us but to help us admonish others in their lives as well. Notice it is the words of Christ, which directly would go to the gospels where we see the words of Christ. It also mentions Psalms, which are in the Old Testament. The teachings of the rest of scripture apply as well because the Spirit of Christ guided the writers to write the books that they wrote.

One important aspect of clarity is that it cuts through the fog and helps us to clearly see the truth in any situation. Clarity can be those "Aha moments" in our life. The scriptures can cut through all the confusion that exists in our world to give us the answers and direction that we need every day. In Hebrews 4:12 it says "For the word of God is living and powerful, and sharper than any two-edged sword, piercing even to the division of soul and spirit, and of joints and marrow, and is a discerner of the thoughts and intents of the heart." The word is compared to a sharp sword that cuts to the truth for us. It not only cuts through the darkness for us, but it can cut deeply and penetrate our very souls and spirits. To walk as a child of the Light, it's vital that we can perceive spiritual truth in our life that goes to the essence of our being itself. The word does this for us.

THE WORD GIVES LIFE

Scripture has the Spirit of Christ in it which gives life, which is stated in John 6:63, which says, "It is the Spirit who gives life; the flesh profits nothing. The words that I speak to you are spirit, and they are life." God's Spirit and the word are the two critical foundations to walking the spiritual life. They go hand in hand. As we saw with meditation, as you ruminate on the word, the Spirit can take those truths and plant them deep within your heart and soul. It lays the firm foundation that Jesus was talking about when He said to build your house on the rock rather than sandy land. Yes, on Jesus, but one way to build your house on Jesus is through incorporating scripture into your life. The Spirit was also present in the word when it inspired the writers of scripture to pen what God wanted to be preserved for humanity. The Bible is literally God-breathed. (II Timothy 2:16, 17) Much like breathing life into Adam, He breathed life into the message of scripture. Life is in the breath, as some may know who have performed CPR on someone or who had CPR performed on them. So the Spirit was present to inspire the scriptures but is also present today in us as we read, meditate, and study the scriptures to activate it into our personal lives today. The Spirit is active both in the past, present, and future applications of the word for people.

The word also gives life because it helps to save and preserve our souls. As James 1:21 says, "Therefore lay aside all filthiness and [d]overflow of wickedness, and receive with meekness the implanted word, which is able to save your souls." Notice that the word is active in helping put aside filthiness and sin. As it embeds in us, it saves and restores our soul to God. Remember, a key aspect of salvation is to restore us to spiritual wholeness in God. You are made whole as you delve into the word daily.

We know we are saved by faith (Galatians 2:15-21) God is the one that gives faith, but what is one way He gives faith to us? The scriptures actually tell us that God uses the word to create faith in a person. As Romans 10:17 says, "So then faith comes by hearing, and hearing by the word of God." The word is not the only way faith may come from God, but it's the primary way that faith comes to a person. Even if a Bible is not directly open when a person embraces Christ, chances are, elements of the word are being conveyed in one form or another to the person. So it's by the word in one form or another. As a person hears the Spirit breathed words of scripture and the Spirit impresses upon the heart the truth of it to the person, a doorway to the heart may be opened to embrace God's Light. This can happen with a highly detailed presentation of the gospel to the person or simply a tiny aspect of the good news touching their hearts. A truth as simple as "God loves you" may reach the heart of the person and they're transformed. This truth that God loves you is, of course, taught in the word.

We have seen that Christ is a life-sustaining presence in our life, like food, water, and air to breathe. The scriptures, too, are like food to us as well. As Mathew 4:4 says "But He answered and said, "It is written, 'Man shall not live by bread alone, but by every word that proceeds from the mouth of God.'" The scriptures are spiritual food to a believer which you've probably heard before. We find both milk and strong meat in the pages of scripture. We should feast on this daily by reading and meditating on it. "Study to show yourself approved". (see II Timothy 2:15) Just as you make physical food a priority each day, make the scriptures a priority for your spiritual sustenance each day.

THE DEPTH OF THE WORD

The word has so many levels of understanding that it may often cause division and confusion for people. I think of the Bible like an onion in that there are so many layers that you can peel back. You will never get to the end of how deep the scriptures go. The Bible is also like a diamond because it has many facets. We had discussed a divine imprint on the book, so this should not come as any surprise. There is so much to study and reflect on. Are there secret codes written in the Bible? I personally don't know. There very well may be, God designed the Bible to be read at so many levels that the truth goes deep and in a million directions. Even without codes, there's enough mystery to be discovered in the pages of scriptures. As it says in Romans 11:33 says "Oh, the depth of the riches both of the wisdom and knowledge of God! How unsearchable are His judgments and His ways past finding out!". This is speaking of God, but where has God sought to lay out his wisdom and knowledge to us? In his word and by his Spirit. If God inspires the scriptures, they are written by an infinite mind that may never be fully understood in this life. There's always more to discover.

What truths people will find as they read the scriptures may vary. No, I'm not speaking of contradictions, but levels of truth.

Everyone is on their own journey in this life, and we are all at different levels. You may discover a truth in a passage that you read years or decades earlier that only became apparent to you now, which is why we should never stop reading the scriptures. You go to the scriptures from a different place as a new believer than you do a mature one. You also come to the scriptures differently based on your life experiences. Your race, gender, ethnicity, and nationality may come into play at times. When I say levels, it's not a simple linear line. You may be more advanced than one person on one issue, but that person may be more advanced in another area. The truths that we find in a genuine sense are always the tip of the iceberg and only scratch the surface.

We can also read the Bible from a more spiritual or literal place. Even though someone may read the scripture more spiritually or allegorically than you, you might just find some deep truths in it, even if you don't agree with their overall interpretation. The same would be true for someone taking passages more literally. Even though you may not agree with all the literalness they come to, you might see a deeper truth there that they hit. We need to be more charitable in how we see other believers. What they see in scripture may not be entirely correct, but they may see some truths you aren't seeing. This is true for them as well. Chances are, no individual, church, denomination, or sect has the corner on all truth or understanding of scripture.

We speak of using Christ as the lens to interpret scripture, which I think is correct. What does Christ perfectly picture for us? Recall, we had said that He is the perfect portrait of love. So ultimately, our lens for the word is through love. We may not always agree, but always be asking if my understanding or another person's understanding is in accordance with love. Love may not get us to the same theological perspective in all cases, but it will get us where we need to be if we are to walk as children of the Light. When the scriptures speak of walking in one accord in Amos 3:3 "Can two walk together, unless they are agreed?", I don't think this is a theological doctrinal agreement so much as that we walk in accord with the transcendent doctrine of love.

THE WORD IN MY LIFE

Like many reading this, I've had times where I was consistently reading the Bible daily, if even a chapter a day. Then there are times where I was not consistently reading the Bible. I don't want you to think I'm this person that reads and studies the Bible for hours each day; I wish that I did. Much of what I wrote in this chapter, I was writing to myself as well as you. Writing this chapter has helped to encourage me to be more in the word.

Besides this chapter, I also wrote an earlier book that compared the Bible with the Near-Death Experience, which is called "Heaven's Truth: The Parallels Between the Bible and the Near-Death Experience". That book strengthened my faith in the scriptures and got me refocused on its importance and value. Writing that book helped to inspire this chapter as a key to walking as a child of the Light.

When I was younger, I spent a lot of time memorizing scriptures. I did it as a new believer and for a Christian school I attended. I remember going to the chapel store of a mega-church I was attending in the 1980s and buying these flashcards with key Bible verses and going through them with my sister Janet to memorize them. Memorization was a wonderful thing for me. Over the years, I still remember most of those verses and they will come back to me from time to time. I may not remember the reference in the Bible. I know the verses. They buried deep within me. They're now great for meditation, reflection, and affirmation. If you've never tried memorizing scripture, I would highly recommend it to you. You can find lists of scriptures with usually only a verse or two on a variety of subjects. If you want inspirational scriptures to memorize, you can find them. If you want promises from the word, they also are easily accessible. You may also find lists of verses about salvation and life in

Christ.

One way that I've found to incorporate the Bible into day-to-day life now is through devotions. You can get very simple ones like "Our Daily Bread" which are free which they will send to you. Our church actually gets "Our Daily Bread" and provides copies to the congregation. If your church doesn't do this, you might encourage them to do so as well. We have discovered that "Our Daily Bread" is online in audio form, which is great too. It will read the devotional story and the scripture readings and say a prayer with you at the end. This can be a good option for the family and individual devotions. We listen as a family to them.

Application

1. Take out your journal and begin listing ways you can integrate the word into your life, besides directly reading it. This may include some ways listed above, such as memorization, audio Bibles, and devotions. Try to come up with at least 10 ways to get scripture into your daily routine. Finally, take at least 2 or 3 you listed and try to do them consistently for the next 21 days to help build a new habit.

2. In your journal, think of at least 5 ways you can incorporate the word into other practices within your life. This could include prayer and meditation. Where else can you apply the word in your life to maximize it for you and others?

5. CENTRALITY
OF LOVE

"Jesus said to him, "'You shall love the Lord your God with all your heart, with all your soul, and with all your mind.' This is the first and great commandment. And the second is like it: 'You shall love your neighbor as yourself.' On these two commandments hang all the Law and the Prophets." (Mathew 22:37-40)

This can't be reiterated enough, love is central to our walking as a child of the Light. You can't walk in the Light without embracing love. It's the essence of our entire faith journey as a believer. Love is the lens through which we view all things. This includes the scriptures themselves. We view Scripture through Christ, but Christ is the embodiment of love, as is God. So love ultimately is our filter to view the scriptures and everything else in our life.

What I'm constantly reminding myself of is to keep returning to love as my center. We can get so caught up in things that really don't matter. Disputes with others, judgments, and theological arguments over this and that, but the only thing that matters is love in the end. If you can keep coming back to that, you will walk in his Light. One place to do this is with your prayers, affirmations, and meditation, along with the word. Theologically, how could anything be more important than love? If you want to understand the nature of God better, you must love because God is love. No fact about God is more important to know and understand.

The gospel is entrenched in love and would make no sense

apart from love. Grace saves us through faith, right? God's grace or unmerited favor is rooted in love. Therefore, John 3:16 says, "For God so loved the world that He gave His only begotten Son, that whoever believes in Him should not perish but have everlasting life." It was love that motivated his grace without question. What is faith? As we have said before, it's trusting or embracing Christ. You can't truly embrace or trust God without love for Him. One key aspect of true faith is repentance. Repentance is to change direction away from sin toward God, or away from that which is contrary to love toward love as God is love.

THE ROYAL LAW OF LOVE

Love is called the royal law in James 2;8 which says, "If you really fulfill the royal law according to the Scripture, "You shall love your neighbor as yourself," you do well;" If you want to genuinely live the Christian life, learn to love more fully and deeply. I've mentioned several times so far how important the fruits of the Spirit are to walking in the Light. The first fruit, of course, is love. The other 8 fruits reflect the first fruit of love. If you think about it, this makes complete sense. If you love, you will have joy and peace. Kindness, patience, and goodness are love in action, as is gentleness. You can't truly love someone and not be faithful, not to God or to another person. Love will help you be more self-controlled and temperate.

Sometimes you will see discussions within the church about whether or not we are under the law. Some say we are under grace. Jesus said, "Do not think that I came to destroy the Law or the Prophets. I did not come to destroy but to fulfill." (Mathew 5:17) How does Jesus fulfill the law ultimately? Yes, by his sacrifice for sin, but why did He do this? It was because of his love. Love fulfills the law. Christ did it this way, isn't it done by believers through love? This is the essence of the royal law of love.

The law itself reflects love. Take the 10 commandments, if

you love God, you will not be worshiping other Gods or putting other things before Him. You will not be disrespectful to his name. If you love others, you will not be stealing, lying, or killing them. This probably seems pretty obvious. The law is good, including the 10 commandments, but the fact that God had to tell you not to kill demonstrates how low humans had sunk within their souls. You've probably seen signs at the store that say "shoplifters will be prosecuted". For most of us, we don't need to be told not to steal. We love and respect others enough that the thought is abhorrent to us. For a few, though, it is necessary that they see this sign. They are operating at a lower level spiritually. Yes, I often reflect on the 10 commandments and how they relate to love and the fruits of the Spirit in my meditation. I like to take them to heart as Jesus taught with adultery, which includes looking upon a woman with lust, or that murder includes hating your brother. (Mathew 5:21-30) I often try to place it in the positive. Ok, I know killing someone is wrong, but what can I do to preserve and honor life more fully? I know stealing is wrong, but how can I respect and be glad for what others have? How can I be happy for them? So the 10 commandments are a beautiful expression of love, and when you extrapolate further, you can find more jewels of wisdom.

THE FULL CIRCLE OF LOVE

Love is much like a chair because it has 3 legs that are essential to have for the chair to work properly. If you remove one leg, the chair will not stand up, it will collapse if you try to sit on it. Even if you have 3 legs but one leg is very weak, the chair will be unstable and may eventually collapse. What are these 3 legs of a chair? You have to love God, your neighbor, and yourself.

These 3 legs work together to support the chair itself, but also work together to make the other 2 even possible. They have a synergistic relationship with each other. If you want to love God better, love your neighbor. If you want to love your neighbor better, love God. If you want to love God and your neighbor better, make sure you also love yourself.

John says in I John 4:20, "If someone says, "I love God," and hates his brother, he is a liar; for he who does not love his brother whom he has seen, [a]how can he love God whom he has not seen?" John doesn't mince any words in this passage. It's impossible to love God and hate your neighbor. You're only fooling yourself if you think otherwise. Love for God starts by loving those around you. Recall what Jesus said, "And the King will answer and say to them, 'Assuredly, I say to you, inasmuch as you did it to one of the least of these My brethren, you did it to Me. (Mathew 25:40). When you love others, you show you love God and Jesus.

You can't walk as a child of the Light if you lack love for others, as it says in I John 2:9 "He who says he is in the light, and hates his brother, is in darkness until now." If you hate your brother, you are in darkness. The essence of hatred is darkness. To walk in the kingdom, you must love.

Love creates oneness between you, God, and other people. It's a bond that cannot be broken. Love gives you the ability to see the dignity in all people and to have compassion for them. You can empathize with them when you love them. You feel a spiritual connection to them. We are all one in this world, yet, so often we cannot see this because we lack love. Love is a powerful, unifying force that makes all things possible.

Some may disagree with me on the importance of loving yourself. I believe this is the starting point, not that you love yourself more than God or others, but that you start with yourself and move outward. When you can truly love yourself, you can let go of bitterness, anger, and unforgiveness you're holding against yourself. Love for yourself makes it much easier to do this when it comes to letting go of anger and bitterness you have toward others. It also makes it easier to forgive them. When I can begin to really see my own humanity and dignity, I can then see it more clearly in others. If you will learn to love yourself, everything else will more easily fall into place, and your walk in the Light will grow by leaps and bounds!

THE NATURE OF LOVE

What truly is the essence of love? We tend to speak of love as one quality, yet are there multiple facets to love? You can speak of loving ice cream. Is that the same as loving your child, or even your dog? We know instinctively that it's not. We only have one word in English for love, which sometimes makes understanding what love is more difficult. In Greek, there are three main words for love. The first one is Eros, which can mean sexual or romantic love. It can also mean to lust. Eros sometimes gets a bad rap, and honestly, it's probably a mixed bag. There is a place for eros, though when you're speaking of a love that is romantic and balanced with the other loves. To have purely sexual love, however, would most likely degrade into lust. This is one reason why developing a broader context within a romantic relationship is so important. You are best served by taking the physical aspects of the relationship slowly. You might be physically attracted to the person but need to take time to get to know the person before you get too physically intimate. This is the best prescription for a lasting relationship. Seek to develop a love that is rooted in genuine care and compassion for the other person. Eros can eventually serve a positive purpose later in a relationship once the relationship has been firmly established. Even there, though, you still need to be careful, and it should always be subservient to the other two loves. (Bible alludes to this Song of Solomon 8:4 don't awaken love too quickly)

The next love is phileo, which is brotherly love. This is a human love that denotes one of companionship. You want to have a strong phileo in your interactions with other people, especially your family. Having a good phileo love is essential to a good marriage and relationship with your children. Phileo by itself can be experienced at varying levels, from deep and mature to more shallow expressions.

The third type of love is agape, which is God's love. It is a perfect, limitless, and unconditional love. This is the type of love that virtually everyone who has had a near-death experience has encountered on the other side when in the presence of God's Light. Can humans love in this way or is it only possible for God to love this way? I believe it is entirely possible to love in this way, but possibly not fully while in this lifetime. We should strive to love in this way. Does agape replace phileo love? I don't believe that it does. Phileo recognizes a context to our love. We love our children in a certain way; we love our spouse in a certain way, etc. It captures these types of love within phileo. Now, can this phileo love we have for them be perfected? Yes! This is the role of agape with our phileo. As we walk in the Light, we deepen our love for others. We can love more unconditionally and expand the limits of our love. With agape, we can also move beyond the immediate context of our love and love them as God loves them. I can love my son as my son, and do so more perfectly, but I can now also see him as God sees him and love in more ways. When we die, the scriptures teach we will not be married, so it's vital that we begin to love our spouses beyond the capacity of spousal love. If you can see your spouse as a friend, companion, and divine light of God that you love, you can expand your love for them. I sometimes think this may be why marriages break up. They have only a narrow romantic spousal love, and when they just aren't feeling or experiencing it like they once did, they leave. If you can diversify that love, you can create a love that lasts a lifetime and beyond.

So I don't see agape love replacing phileo but, purifying it; perfecting it; expanding it; and going beyond its more narrow focus. We get an interesting play between phileo and agape in John 21:15-17. This is where Jesus asks Peter 3 times if he loves Him. Jesus uses the word agape to ask Peter if he loves Him. Peter answers that he phileos Him. The third time, Jesus uses Peter's word of phileo when asking if Peter loves Him. There are so many interpretations of this passage, but I think the point of what I said above can apply. Jesus is asking if He loves Him perfectly with God's love. Peter can only commit to a human brotherly love at this time. Jesus then accepts this and has him affirm that He loves him as a brother for the third time. The 3 times of questioning may go to Peter, denying Him 3 times. This may have been a restoration of Peter's call and ministry in Christ. We know from both scripture and tradition that Peter would die for Him. He says that He will die for Him in verse 19. This indicates that Peter would get to where his love would be so deep and perfected that he would give up everything, including life itself, to serve Christ. In this, Peter will have moved to the realm of apape. Yet, He will still love Christ in a phileo way as a brother as well, just in a more exalted form of phileo. Tradition says that Peter requested to be crucified upside down because He didn't feel worthy to die in the same what that his Lord did, further pointing to his agape love for Jesus.[18]

SACRIFICIAL LOVE

Probably the most famous verse in the Bible is John 3:16, which says, "For God so loved the world that He gave His only begotten Son, that whoever believes in Him should not perish but have everlasting life." The love in this verse is agape, which is God's perfect, unconditional love. This love was given to the entire world without exception. The word world here is cosmos which means the earth.[19] Yes, God's love was showered upon every person who ever lived or ever will live on earth, but this gift of his Son covers all of creation as well. There is a creational restoration that is going to take place. Colossians 1:20 says, "and by Him to reconcile all things to Himself, by Him, whether things on earth or things in heaven, having made peace through the blood of His cross." God's plan was to restore everything by the cross. Romans 8:20,21 "20 For the creation was subjected to futility, not willingly, but because of Him who subjected it in hope; 21 because the creation itself also will be delivered from the bondage of [f]corruption into the glorious liberty of the children of God." The creation itself was affected by the fall into sin, but God was going to rescue that as well. God's sacrifice was for everyone and everything. When Jesus died, there was a tremendous explosion of love that covered this world, an explosion we can't fully understand, but everything was changed. The veil of the temple was ripped in twain, symbolizing the old system had passed and we were in a new one. (Matthew 27; 51)

Notice in John 3:16 that God gave up his son. How many of us would give up our child for others like this? God made the supreme sacrifice for us to demonstrate his love. When you consider the Trinity, God actually gave a piece of Himself in this sacrifice as well. We don't fully understand the trinity, but it might be like us giving up a limb for someone else. We all admire those that do organ donation. God gave us a piece of Himself so that we might live. He also shed his blood for us, which is like getting a blood donation on top of it all. It was through the blood that we gained the remission of sins. (Mathew 26:28)

We know that the highest expression of love is that of sacrificial love. This is why we pay honor to those that laid down their lives for our nation. We also remember the sacrifices previous generations made so that we could have a better life today. This is at the heart of how we love as parents with our children. John 15:13 says, "Greater love has no one than this, than to lay down one's life for his friends." Jesus laid down his life for us and thus revealed the kind of love He had for us.

Would it have been possible in God's love to simply forgive our sins without having to sacrifice his son on the cross for our sins? Hebrews 9:22 says, "And according to the law almost all things are [a]purified with blood, and without shedding of blood there is no [b]remission." (KJV). God has set up a universal law that there must be a payment for sin. One can think of this as a cosmic balancing of the books. If you acquire a negative balance, you have to have something that offsets it to bring things into balance. This is also what the law of reaping and sowing is about. Could God have set things up differently? Possibly, but this is speculation. Had He done this, we never would have been able to see how profound his love for us really is. Without the balancing of scales, we never would have understood the harm our sins cause God and others.

As amazing as dying for a friend would be, one could imagine possibly dying for them. Romans 5:7 says, "For scarcely for a righteous man will one die; yet perhaps for a good man someone would even dare to die." God's love went even further than one dying for a friend though, Christ's sacrificial love for us runs so deep that He was willing to die for us even while we were steeped in sin. Romans goes on to say in verse 8 to say "But God demonstrates His own love toward us, in that while we were still sinners, Christ died for us." God loves us not for what we have done, but for who He is, which is love itself. This verse, like John 3:16, is inclusive of all people, for everyone has sinned. Early in Romans, it said in 3:23, "for all have sinned and fall short of the glory of God," So God loved the entire world and died for it while it was still in sin. No one is above the love of God. No one is without hope. It's a matter of embracing this love yourself.

LOVE COVERS A MULTITUDE OF SINS

We know that Adam's sin brought death into the world as it says in Romans 5:12 "Therefore, just as through one man sin entered the world, and death through sin, and thus death spread to all men, because all sinned". The word Adam means man, so of course, it refers to his individual sin but also the collective sin of the entire human race. We continued this downward spiral with our own sins. You have both the collective sin of humanity and our own individual sins that bring us down into further darkness. We reap the consequences of our sin as well as the sins of humanity. This may not seem fair, but we're all in the same boat, and my actions affect you, and your actions affect me. We have the cumulative effect of sin that grows over generations with the ramifications being passed down. If this was the end of the story, it would be quite a gloomy picture, but it didn't end there.

As powerful as sin is, there is something more potent that can wipe it out. Love itself covers sin, which is contrary to love. Here, it was a specific and authoritative expression of love that was at the cross. In verse 15 of the same chapter, it says, "But the free gift is not like the [e]offense. For if by the one man's offense many died, much more the grace of God and the gift by the grace of the one Man, Jesus Christ, abounded to many." Not only does God's grace through the cross cover sin, but it's way more powerful than sin itself. Notice the words "much more" speaking of the grace that wiped out sin. No amount of sin, whether it be the collective sin of humanity or our own personal sin can ever be enough to overpower his love. No amount of sin can ever keep a person from finding life in Christ, or for his plan for the world to be accomplished. As verse 18 says, "Therefore, as through [h]one man's offense judgment came to all men, resulting in condemnation, even so through one[i] Man's righteous act the free gift came to all men, resulting in justification of life." The gift of life and his love comes upon all people. Paul makes a similar parallel in I Corinthians 15:22, which says, "For as in Adam all die, even so in Christ all shall be made alive." In Christ or by Christ, all shall be made alive. God, because of His love showered at the cross, is not holding our sins against us. As it says in II Corinthians 5:19, "that is, that God was in Christ reconciling the world to Himself, not [d]imputing their trespasses to them, and has committed to us the word of reconciliation." Not only is our sin not being held to our account, but He is reconciling the world unto himself. The debt in our spiritual bank account has been paid, and He is now making deposits in it daily!

We can see how love covers sin at the cross, but we're given the same pattern in our own lives. I Peter 4:8 says, "And above all things have fervent love for one another, for "love will cover a multitude of sins." Love can wipe out all sins, no matter how many or how great the sin is. As we move in fervent love for others, the love grows within us and so does its power. The more you love, the more sin it can cover. I've even heard of people through Christ's love being able to forgive a murderer who killed their child. If a parent can forgive the murder of his or her child, then anything is possible through love. Love is the mechanism that makes forgiveness possible. If you want to forgive, and you know you should, you need to develop more love. This is where prayer and meditation on love come in. God, through his Spirit, can fill you with greater love. Remember, we talked about God giving continual blessings throughout our lives? This is one of them. Being given an outpouring of love is actually more important than a healing miracle or the gifts of the Spirit. The best gift you can get is love. Love will change your perspective on everything. Love will give you the desire and ability to walk in the Light, including forgiveness.

Love will unlock the other fruits of the Spirit, such as peace, joy, gentleness, and kindness, which will help you let the sins of others go, as well as be able to forgive yourself. Love will give you a new perspective on life and everything in it. Love grows into the heart of compassion. When you can feel compassion for others that have harmed you, your world, and their world, will be radically changed.

LOVE IS THE MOST IMPORTANT THING

We know that the entire law is established on love. As Jesus said in Mathew 22:37-40.

> **37** Jesus said to him, "'You shall love the Lord your God with all your heart, with all your soul, and with all your mind.' **38** This is *the* first and great commandment. **39** And *the* second *is* like it: 'You shall love your neighbor as yourself.' **40** On these two commandments hang all the Law and the Prophets."

The law itself reflects love and is an outgrowth of love. The law came into being because we had sunk so low into sin and darkness that we needed a guide on how to live in love. This guide needed to be expanded as time went on throughout the Old Testament. Not only is the law built on love, but so are the rest of the teachings in the Old Testament which came after and before the law. The history of the Old Testament reflects love and should be our guide in reading it. This is, of course, is true of the New Testament as well. In fact, the New Testament is more explicit on the importance of love and more fully reflects love. The Bible is a progressive revelation of God but is also a progressive expression of who God is. As the Bible unfolds, we get a clearer picture of who God is.

Paul made the point abundantly clear in I Corinthians 13:1-4 that without love, nothing else matters

> If I speak in the tongues of men and of angels, but have not love, I am a noisy gong or a clanging cymbal. ² And if I have prophetic powers, and understand all mysteries and all knowledge, and if I have all faith, so as to remove mountains, but have not love, I am nothing. ³ If I give away all I have, and ᵈif I deliver up my body to be burned,¹ but have not love, I gain nothing. (ESV)

Love Is More Important Than Miracles

Notice that love is more important than tongues in this verse. Love takes precedence over signs and wonders, which may surprise some people. People in Jesus' day were always looking for a miracle to be performed to authenticate Him being the Christ. Jesus would never perform a miracle simply to prove Himself or satisfy those seeking a sign. There was always a context to his miracles. Yes, the miracles proved He was who He claimed to be, the Son of God, but they served a larger purpose. Jesus' miracles were done primarily to show forth compassion and love. The miracles served the interest of love itself. This was also true of the miracles performed by the Apostles. The miracles were not "magic tricks" to amaze the crowds, but ultimately served the interest of love. When someone is healed of an ailment by God, that person is being shown God's love. Not that when a person isn't healed, God loves them less, He may have another purpose to be fulfilled in not healing them.

We have entire movements built on performing the signs and wonders of God. We have churches that focus the vast majority of their time doing healing and miracle services. There are churches and movements that have made speaking in tongues a prerequisite of showing you are filled with the Holy Spirit. There's nothing wrong with praying for a miracle or healing. I believe God does miracles today and has done them over the centuries. They aren't supposed to be the focus of the church though, the primary focus of the church and individual believers should be love. Love really is the greatest miracle. A transformed life goes way beyond a temporal healing of the body. We see the divisions that some of these movements can cause. We see hucksters that come in claiming to do miracles that often have ulterior motives. This is allowed to happen because we have the wrong focus and because God doesn't do miracles on command to entertain and amuse us. If someone is sick or needs prayer for a healing, by all means, pray, but remember, the ultimate goal in praying is out of a heart of love and compassion.

Love Is More Important Than Theology

Notice it says "all mysteries and all knowledge" in the verses above. Like with miracles, there have been churches and movements built around having an exacting theology that is completely pure and perfect. They have creeds and statements that are preeminent in their churches. If you don't align with their theology on very specific points, you're viewed as not even being a Christian and probably not going to heaven. Do I hold certain doctrines and beliefs? Yes, I believe in the Trinity and the deity of Jesus. I believe in baptism and many other things. But I'm not saved because my understanding and knowledge are perfect. I'm saved through his love and by embracing that love. Remember, love, covers a multitude of sins. Don't you think love can cover an "improper" view of the trinity? Most of the things people get so uptight about, much of the early church wouldn't have understood today, anyway. Our theological understanding has evolved over the centuries as people pondered and studied the scriptures. A single verse can not grasp much of the deep theology but takes extensive study to see it if you can see it. So why be so dogmatic? It's clear to me that many display the fruits of the Spirit yet, would not align with many doctrinal statements or confessions. If they walk in the Spirit, how can they not be a brother or sister? When Philip baptized the Ethiopian Eunuch, He only asked him if he believed that Jesus was the Christ, the Son of God. He didn't ask him for an extensive laundry list to "test" his faith. We should bear that in mind. (Acts 8:36-38)

Not that studying theology has no value. It has tremendous value. We do want to understand the nature of our creator better and to grasp all his truths. I have enjoyed the study of theology over the years and had many interesting doctrinal discussions with people. I've just come to realize that love is to be our primary focus. Remember that doctrine means teaching. Love is the doctrine of supreme importance, the one we need to keep refocusing ourselves on.

Faith, Hope, and Love

In I Corinthians 13, which we cited above, Paul goes on in verse 13 to say, "And now abide faith, hope, love, these three; but the greatest of these is love." We have three important keys in our walk in the Light, but love is the most important one. I always found this verse to be odd when I was younger. In church, we often hear that faith is the most important thing to have. How is it that love is actually more important? As we have said earlier, without love rooting our faith, it's only going to be a mental assent to a set of beliefs. Love helps you to embrace Christ with all your heart.

James said in James 2:26, "For as the body without the spirit is dead, so faith without works is dead also." We are not saved by faith and works, but by a faith that works. How is it that we receive a faith that works in our life? Through love. Love is the agent that activates the faith in our life. When you operate from a heart of love for God and others, works is second nature to you. It freely flows from you. It isn't something that becomes a drudgery for you. It's not something you have to do, it's something you get to do. You enjoy serving God and others when it's done in love.

THE POWER OF LOVE

We can never underestimate the power of love to transform a person's life.

We Are Made New By His Love

In II Corinthians 5:17, it says, "Therefore, if anyone is in Christ, he is a new creation; old things have passed away; behold, all things have become new." To be in Christ is to be in his love because Christ, as is his Father, is love and embodies everything about love. So it is this love that transforms everything in our lives when we embrace it. We become something entirely new, a new creation or being within us. It changed every aspect of our life. We often hear the phrase "She has a new lease on life" or "He's turned over a new leaf". These phrases really don't fully capture what has happened with this new creation life in love. Really, we got an entirely new leaf. We received a brand new life.

This transformative power is potent enough to change anyone. You can hear powerful testimonies of people that were delivered from drug addiction, alcoholism, sex addictions, and crime. Even murderers have found a completely new way of living in this love. Think of the Apostle Paul, who was a murderer of Christians before his spiritually transformative experience on the road to Damascus. We have examples in our own day of such transformation. Karla Faye Tucker, who viciously killed two people with a pickaxe, was completely changed when she embraced Christ in prison. She was eventually executed, but rest assured, she went to a place of perfect peace and love.

Many might be saying, I'm not a drug addict, and I've never killed anyone. What does this have to do with me? The point is that if such a person above can find this transformational power, anyone can. We've all sinned. Romans 3:23 says, "for all have sinned and fall short of the glory of God," We have intuitively recognized that we have not lived up to what we should have. We know we don't even today. We know that we have done wrong and have flaws. So we, too, need this transformation.

His love Is Poured Out Upon Us

Recall, we had talked about in an earlier chapter that God can shower us with the blessings of love, compassion, peace, etc. throughout our lifetime. It's not just a one time blessing or a second or third special blessing, but one that can happen daily and anytime. In Romans 5:5 it says "Now hope does not disappoint, because the love of God has been poured out in our hearts by the Holy Spirit who was given to us." Love is poured out when we come to Christ but is continually poured out. We are transformed within our soul from the moment we receive Christ, but often the impact in our lives is not immediate. It's a gradual process over days, weeks, years, and even a lifetime. Occasionally, you will receive immediate transformation in something, but this is rare. Everything we need is there to fully walk in love and more blessings are being added, but it may take a while to notice the drink offering in the cup as it's being poured. This is the sanctification process. It's our outward conscious expression of faith manifesting what is already there, deep within our souls.

We Will Be Known By Our Love

We often think people will know that they are a person of faith by religious symbols we wear or carry. If they see my cross necklace; if they see my Jesus loves me T-shirt, if they see my big leather Bible with the gold pages, then they will know that I'm a Christian. Sometimes we think if we speak religiously using religious phrases or quoting scripture to them, then they will know I'm a believer. There's nothing wrong with any of those things, but it's not actually the primary way people will know you follow Christ. In John 13:34, 35 it says, "**34** A new commandment I give to you, that you love one another; as I have loved you, that you also love one another. **35** By this all will know that you are My disciples, if you have love for one another." The love that you show towards others speaks volumes as to who you are. If you want to share your faith, do so through your love. Religious symbols and expressions will actually repel many people if they don't see the love within you. If you use those things to support love and, in conjunction with love, it's a different story.

You Can Do All Things With Love

In I Corinthians 13:7, it says love "bears all things, believes all things, hopes all things, endures all things". Love gives you the power to completely walk as a child of the Light. It empowers you to do what you need to do to walk in the Light. Love gives you the faith to believe that all things are possible. Love gives you the ability to have faith in Christ in the first place. When you have love in your heart, you can then trust God and others as you go through life.

Love gives you hope to live each day with joy and peace. Love also gives you the hope of a brighter future in this life and in the life to come. When you have hope, you can move forward in power to do everything you want to do and know you should do to walk in the Light. When you lack hope, nothing seems possible or worth doing, so hope in love is essential to walk in Christ.

Love gives you the ability to endure anything that comes at you in life. Christians in the New Testament and over the centuries were able to endure imprisonment, torture, persecution, and even death because of the love they had in their hearts for God. We may not face such things, or at least to the same extent, but it can give us the power to endure a cancer diagnosis, losing a job, or the death of a loved one. If we do face any persecution, we can endure that as well.

One of my favorite verses is Philippians 4:13, which says, "I can do all things through [f]Christ who strengthens me". If Christ is love, put the word love in for just a moment. I can do all things through [f]Love who strengthens me. Through God's love, all things become possible for us. I think of love like the engine of a car when it comes to walking in the Light. If a car had no engine, it can't run. The engine is essential. Since we have love as our engine, let's seek to build the biggest, most powerful love engine we can! Love is also like the fuel that runs the car. With no gas in the tank, you're not moving. Fuel up on his love daily. Love is the battery of the car as well. You need the battery to spark the engine to work. We need his spark of love to get things moving in our walk with Him.

LOVE IN FELLOWSHIP

Most of us have heard that we should not forsake the assembling together our entire Christian life. In Hebrews 10:25, it says, "not forsaking the assembling of ourselves together, as *is* the manner of some, but exhorting *one another,* and so much the more as you see the Day approaching."

Fellowship Is A Point Of Opportunity

Many take this verse as a point of duty in our walk with Christ, and it is, of course, but it's really so much more than that. Try to see it not so much as a duty but as an opportunity, though. Why is that? Because as you fellowship with others, you open yourself up each time to a whole host of blessings. The blessing can be for you. It can also be an opportunity to bless others which intern can be the biggest blessing to you! One thing we don't think of is that as you become present in others' lives, it may give them an opportunity to bless and serve you, which may be exactly what you need but may also be exactly what they need. When you have such blessings coming to both you and others at the same time, you have a divine appointment set by God in that situation. This opens the door to the perfecting of love for everyone. Don't miss your chance to participate in one of God's divine appointments if you can help it! God may have a special message or person to minister to waiting for you. God may have a special job for you that day. You should always go to fellowship with the expectation of receiving something of great value from fellowship. You may also receive blessings just by seeing what He does for others as well.

God designed fellowship because He created us to be social creatures. We were never intended to be islands unto ourselves. From the very beginning, God said, "It is not good for man to be alone" (Genesis 2:18). The direct context was within marriage but really has application in virtually all human relationships. You notice throughout scripture, fellow believers are referred to as brothers and sisters. We are all part of a special spiritual family. As a family, we should love each other with our time, among other things. Time is probably the most important aspect of developing loving relationships, regardless of the context. We certainly know this to be true within a marriage or with our children. They don't know how much you love them until they see you spending time with them. Half the battle in life is simply showing up.

Music In Fellowship

There are several elements to worship where love can be expressed both toward God and each other. One of them is in worship songs. The music can move our hearts in love and helps us to become more loving in that moment with each other. Music has a way of bonding people together. We see this even within many secular contexts, such as at ball games. Paul says in Ephesians 5:19 "speaking to one another in psalms and hymns and spiritual songs, singing and making melody in your heart to the Lord," Music has a way of speaking to us and is a way we can communicate deeply with each other. It's also a way to express deep love to God. One thing to do from time to time is not just go through the motions of singing, but take time to really listen to the music. Notice the words, take them to heart. Ponder them as they are being sung. You may not go to a church where people tend to close their eyes and put their hands up, but allow yourself to close your eyes occasionally and just briefly meditate on the music. I do this from time to time. Notice what the songs are saying to God and about our relationship with each other. I'm telling you, it can take an "old boring hymn" and breathe new life into it. When some of these older hymns were written, a lot of heart went into them, they did have deep meaning for the authors. We just become too familiar with it and sing it with no thought. It becomes an empty ritual for us.

Fellowship Of Praise

Another aspect of fellowship is to give praise and gratitude to God. We do this in music but also in the teaching and service within the church. Remember, one key to meditation was gratitude. We want to affirm and express our gratitude toward God, which will help us grow in love and to become more connected to love. This will help us grow in love with one another as well. You can praise and thank God for the people He has put around you and blessed you with.

Fellowship In Prayer

Remember, we had discussed how prayer together can be a way to practice communion with each other? Praying together in fellowship can also help to grow us together in love and compassion and is a way to bear one another's burdens. Praying together intensifies the spiritual energy going to and coming from God. A single stick by itself is only so strong, but when you bundle a bunch together, the strength vastly increases. This concept is actually taught in the Bible. (see Ecclesiastes 4:12).

We're strong in virtually every way you can think of together.

Remembering Christ In Communion

One of the most important ways that we fellowship together is in the practice of taking communion. With communion, we remember the supreme act of love shown on the cross that has the power to wash away our sins. As I've said before, a massive explosion of love that forever changed the world took place on the cross. This action changed the way God relates to us and how we relate to Him. It also affects how we relate to each other because now we are all one at the cross. All former divisions are gone. This makes the act of communion of vital importance, as it gives us a powerful way to remember the cross. It's what Christ gave us Himself. It has a connection to the Old Testament, as the Israelites remembered Passover with a meal of bread and wine in it. Jesus is the ultimate Passover lamb for the entire world.

Jesus said this is "my body and blood, take eat" (Luke 22). This is a point of contention. Is this the literal body and blood of Jesus? I don't personally believe it is. Others can disagree with this. I do believe, though, there is a special presence of Christ when we partake beyond just a memorial service. Jesus" presence and power are manifest in a way spiritually that we may not completely understand in communion.

The Three Es In Fellowship

Fellowship allows for what I call the three Es of edification, encouragement, and exhortation. The three all overlap and have much in common, but there are some differences emphasized to them. Edification has to do with building up and improving up generally through instruction in good teaching. This typically happens through the direct teaching or sermon which centers around the teaching of the word, but can also happen during songs, discussions, and even by observing others. Sometimes the best teacher is by example. Encouragement is giving someone support and confidence. We understand what encouragement is, letting people know that through Christ, all things are possible in their life. They can get through this, they can overcome whatever obstacle is in front of them. This mountain in their life can be removed. Exhortation is encouraging someone to do something, go forth in your life and show love, pray each day for God's help, or serve others, for example, It's quite possible that within one teaching you can have all three going on at the same time.

Sharing With Others In Fellowship

Fellowship is also a time for sharing our gifts and talents that God has given us to serve others. This is a powerful way to walk in love and often you do feel that love. Sometimes God has set us up so that we are the objects of someone else's gifts of service. That's perfectly fine. We need both parts. We can be blessed in both roles and should seek to participate in both roles.

Formal And Informal Fellowship

The question arises, can the fellowship mentioned above only occur within the church service? That is to say, a formal official church meeting? Really, we are the church as his people. The building is not the church, it's an assembly or meeting hall. I believe that one of the principal places such fellowship with other believers takes place is in the formal assembling each week together. Can it occur in other contexts as well, though? Absolutely! Jesus said, "For where two or three are gathered together in My name, I am there in the midst of them." (Mathew 18:20) Anytime you have believers together, there is always an opportunity to fellowship. The building or location is not really that important, the early church met in homes. Later, they met in the catacombs. You could even hold formal assemblies in homes, parks, rented hotels, etc. today. The difference obviously between a formal assembly and just informally meeting for fellowship is that formal meetings are scheduled to meet at a set time each week, or multiple times. They tend to have all or most of the elements of fellowship going on mentioned above.

An informal fellowship may be more sporadic and impromptu, it may only have a single element like bible study or a few elements. Both the formal and informal assembling have value. I would encourage you not to forsake either. Sometimes the informal fellowship times allow you to get to know someone better on a personal level.

Fellowship With Unbelievers

Does fellowship only occur within the context of believers? I don't believe this is the case. You can have wonderful discussions with those that don't believe. This can feed your soul and help you to grow in love for them. You understand where people are coming from and can better minister to them. I'm not in any way talking about engaging in sin or "loving the world". We don't love the world in terms of its sins, but we do love the people in the world. Jesus fellowshipped with all types, including prostitutes and tax collectors. I'm sure He dialogued with them often about his teachings as He did with his own disciples. Paul went to Mars hill to discuss truth with the philosophers of his day. (see Acts 17) When fellowshipping with those that don't yet believe, this could include a direct presentation of the gospel but can just be sharing truths in love. It could just be showing love. That could be as simple as having a cup of coffee with someone and allowing them to tell you how they're feeling.

MY JOURNEY WITH LOVE AT THE CENTER

I've been a Christian for over 40 years now and like most Christians within the evangelical world, the primary focus of my Christian life had been theology. To have pure "doctrine" is paramount in most evangelical circles, even today. This usually turns out to be true when they say that it isn't the case. Salvation rests ultimately in most of their minds on a proper understanding of a few theological truths. For some, the laundry list is longer than for others. This idea can cause a great deal of fear and anger within the church. We fear those that are just too "beyond the pale" of how we understand the scriptures. We also begin to fear when some believers "stray" just a little too far in their questioning of things. To some extent, this focus on dogma goes back even to many of the church fathers. It creates a tension between our belief in the importance of love and our belief in the importance of good theology.

For about the last 15 years, I've made love the central point of my walk with Christ. I've consciously committed to it. It has taken years for love to become a genuine focal point, however. It's a gradual process, like most things we have discussed. Once you begin fully grasping God's unconditional love within your being, it becomes easier. Can you see God's love running so deep that even someone in a cult could be saved? Can you fathom a Mormon or Jehovah's Witness being a child of God because he or she deeply loves God and Christ within their heart? This in no way is an endorsement of their respective organizations or any organizations for that matter. It's not an endorsement of their theology. My point is that through love, anyone can embrace Christ and that God is big enough to see through less than perfect theology to love and embrace them back. If they deeply love Christ within their heart, they don't have a different Christ, but may simply have a different understanding of how it all works out. Kind of like two children that lost their mother. The younger child might have some faulty ideas that the older child doesn't, but one would never say, oh, they had two different mothers. God loves us all, even if we do have faulty ideas.

I should give a note of caution. I recognize that some religious groups may have a high degree of authoritarianism. Such groups take authority away from the individual to govern their lives or to spiritually seek to discern God or the Bible for themselves. This authoritarianism generally uses high levels of control and manipulation. They tend to be quite exclusive and see themselves as the only ones going to heaven or having a special relationship with God that no one outside the group possesses. This authoritarianism is not in accordance with love. Still, it may be possible for individuals within such an organization to be genuine followers of the Light within their hearts. God may even use such organizations to help lead them into some truth or may use it as a stepping stone in the person's spiritual development. If someone was to ask me if they should join or remain in such an organization, I would recommend personally that they do not. Remember too, one must be careful of authoritarian mindsets that can set in even outside of an organization. Love doesn't seek to control or put force on others. This is a key to my journey. I do admit that seeing ministries and churches that seem to have all the answers can be appealing to many. I have felt the draw before but never surrender your right to go to God for yourself, as well as to study scripture prayerfully. Love recognizes the dignity of all people and never seeks to set one person or an elite group over others.

As I have said before, I enjoy the study of theology and have certain beliefs that I hold to, but they're always secondary to love in importance. Much of it is academic, I find it an interesting pursuit of study. I never live in fear that someone is going to hell because they don't "get it right". Nor does it anger me when I come into a disagreement with someone over theology. We are all on a journey in this life, which includes our current understanding of how we view God. We need to learn empathy and compassion for where people are right now.

Application

1. Take out your journal and begin listing all the times you felt profound love in your lifetime. Take time over the next few days in prayer and meditation to focus on these profound moments.

2. In your journal, think of what your journey with love has been in your walk with Christ. Has it been or become the most important factor in your walk? Be honest. What other factors, if any, have been more important than love for you in your walk?

3. What can you do in your life to make love more of a focal point in your life? Be specific and write them down.

6. KINDNESS
IN ACTION

"Therefore, as God's chosen people, holy and dearly loved, clothe yourselves with compassion, kindness, humility, gentleness and patience." (Colossians 3:12 NIV)

In the preceding chapter, we discussed love, which is the most important thing to have if we are to walk as a child of the Light. What is love, though, and what does it look like? Is love more than just a warm fuzzy feeling? Of course, it is! Love is something we carry within our hearts and souls. Kindness is one of the principal ways we demonstrate love and can see love. Kindness is love in action. It's taking what is in our hearts and putting it out there in the real world. It's something concrete and tangible we can see. Kindness is like the machine that reads our vitals. Kindness sends a message to the world that we have love. Can we have love without kindness? Possibly, but it would most likely not be a strong and vibrant love because when love runs deep, it wants to be actively engaged? Can you have kindness without love? I believe this is possible as well. You could show kindness out of a sense of duty or to impress people. In most cases, though, love is usually the main motivating factor. Duty and impressing others will only carry you so far. I think it's also possible that as we show kindness, our love will begin to develop and grow. It's hard to serve others in kindness and not begin to feel some love for them. So love motivates kindness, but kindness also helps love to grow.

The scripture anticipates that we develop a love so strong

that it causes us to act. James 1:22, 23 says, "But be doers of the word, and not hearers only, deceiving yourselves. 23 For if anyone is a hearer of the word and not a doer, he is like a man observing his natural face in a mirror;". People need to be able to see your love if you are to be an effective witness for the Light. Love that is truly worth anything will be set in motion.

Kindness can be grand things, like starting a soup kitchen in your town or a ministry to feed thousands in Africa, but it can also be small and subtle things as well. A smile, a kind word of encouragement, or bringing a glass of cold water to someone can show kindness. Most of the time, it will be the minor acts of kindness that we can so easily do. We don't need a ton of money, resources, or connections to show small acts of kindness. If it's done from a heart of love, it can be just as important in the sight of God as the more grandiose actions.

Kindness, like love, is a fruit of the Holy Spirit. Closely connected to kindness is goodness. Good deeds, whether great or small, are an act of kindness. Goodness is broader than kindness, but kindness is a significant way we can show goodness to others. We tend to think of a good. person as someone who is kind.

GOD SETS THE EXAMPLE BY SHOWING KINDNESS

God sets the example of kindness for us in all that He has done and provided for us. In Ephesians 2:7, it says, "that in the ages to come He might show the exceeding riches of His grace in His kindness toward us in Christ Jesus." We find the primary expression of kindness given by God in sending Jesus to earth. God sent his son to personally pay for our sins and reconcile us through the work of Christ. Christ was in the world reconciling it to Himself. (See II Corinthians 5:19). God didn't just send a message of good rules to live by but gave Jesus as our example of how we should live in addition to paying for our sins. He sent his son as an ambassador for Himself to us. This level of kindness is amazing, to say the least.

By Christ, we could be perfected and find complete joy and peace within Him. The kindness through Christ will be continually being revealed through the ages. It starts now and goes through all eternity. We don't even know the full extent of his kindness yet. I Corinthians 2:9 says, "Eye has not seen, nor ear heard, Nor have entered into the heart of man The things which God has prepared for those who love Him." (quoting Isaiah 64:4) We will see an unfolding of God's great kindness through eternity. What a magnificent God we serve!

God's kindness is better than anything else as it says in Psalms 63:3 "Because Your lovingkindness *is* better than life, My lips shall praise You.". Nothing in this life can compare to the kindness that God showers on us. In fact, anything we have in life is directly or indirectly a result of God's loving-kindness being shown upon us. Whether it be the sun shining, good health, or enough to eat. God makes all things possible for us. Therefore, we should have an attitude of gratitude and thank God in all things. Even the difficult things are placed in our life to ultimately be for our good. It might be there to teach us a lesson or get our attention.

KINDNESS TOWARD THE POOR

There are literally hundreds of verses related to helping the poor, but we will just look at a few key verses. In Luke 6:30 it says, "Give to everyone who begs from you, and from one who takes away your goods do not demand them back." (ESV) I really like how the English Standard translates this verse because it uses the word "beg" which denotes specifically that the person is most likely poor. Most translations use the word "ask". The basic attitude that we should have is to give from a kind and generous heart, expecting nothing back in return. Simply showing love and knowing that you could help someone in need is payment enough. The true mark of kindness is simply to show love with no ulterior motive in mind. When you can give freely, expecting nothing in return, your heart will be truly free and you will be able to more fully manifest the fruits of the Spirit. This is vital to walking as a child of the Light. This can be one of the most profound ways we can shift the paradigm in how we view others as well as ourselves.

We need to show our love for the poor with our actions. I John 3:18 says, "My little children, let us not love in word or in tongue, but in deed and in truth." It's not enough to simply think kind thoughts or speak kind words, but kind deeds must follow them up in many cases. There may be times when a simple kind word or gesture is enough, but sometimes it may require more of us, especially with the poor. James 2:16 says, "and one of you says to them, "Depart in peace, be warmed and filled,' but you do not give them the things which are needed for the body, what *does it* profit?" We can't always help everyone in need, but if it's within our power, we should do what we can with what we have. We should show kindness in everything we do. Showing kindness to the poor can take many forms. It can be a person we see on the streets. The person could be a neighbor. It may also include giving generously to charitable organizations. Even when you see the bell ringing with the Salvation Army at Christmas, you should seek to give something if you have it. If your church has outreaches to the poor within the community, nationally, or globally, you can support that. If your church doesn't currently assist the poor in some way, encourage them to do so.

We should have eagerness and excitement when helping those in need. Paul said in Galatians 2:9, 10 "and when James, [a]Cephas, and John, who seemed to be pillars, perceived the grace that had been given to me, they gave me and Barnabas the right hand of fellowship, that we *should go* to the Gentiles and they to the circumcised. *They desired* only that we should remember the poor, the very thing which I also was eager to do." Notice that the Other Apostles were specifically thinking of the poor when they offered fellowship to Paul. This was the only request made by the other Apostles to Paul. Paul's response was important as well. This was exactly what Paul was excited to do!

Showing kindness to the poor is an essential element of living out our faith.

How can we show the same type of enthusiasm toward helping the poor that Paul had? Start by allowing your heart to be filled with love and compassion. This is one area you can meditate on during your meditations. You can see those being helped by what you gave and feel the joy that giving can bring. If you gave a dollar to the Salvation Army at Christmas, see that dollar bringing a gift to a child or giving someone a Christmas meal. With giving today often being so distant from our view, we need to remind ourselves of why it's important to give even if remote.

In Colossians 3:12, it says, "Since God chose you to be the holy people he loves, you must clothe yourselves with tenderhearted mercy, kindness, humility, gentleness, and patience." (NLT) This verse is telling us to clothe ourselves with kindness as well as other qualities such as gentleness and patience. Our kindness should adorn our presence and be something that everyone can clearly see in our lives.

God has told us He will reward those that show compassion to the poor. Proverbs 19:17 says, "Whoever is kind to the poor lends to the Lord, and he will reward them for what they have done." We shouldn't do our good deeds to be rewarded later, but this is something that God says that He will do. It's an added benefit to what we already received by the good feeling we get when we help others. Maybe part of the reward in heaven is to have the opportunity to see and feel how the person we helped felt as they experienced it. So we get the joy of knowing that we helped, but the joy of actually experiencing our help. You might also feel the intense love that God felt in that moment that you served that person.

Is helping the poor the sum total of our walk with Christ? There was a doctrine that was popular in the early part of the 20th century called the social gospel. It basically said that the gospel is only shown through the aid to the poor. This certainly misses the Great Commission and the importance of sharing Christ with people. Another problem is that assisting the poor and those in need should not be reduced down to exclusively helping with physical needs like food, shelter, clothing, etc. There are many ways a person can be poor. Financial assistance is one important area, but not the only area. People may need help materially, emotionally, physically, or spiritually. We should seek to show kindness to those in need within all these realms. Helping a person spiritually can include sharing Christ and giving them the love and hope that He offers. It may also include making disciples of people. The areas all interconnect, and often as you help in one area, you may help in another area. As you show compassion to the poor in meeting their material needs, you may also open a door to reach them with their spiritual and emotional needs as well.

KINDNESS TOWARD THE WEAK AMONG US

One way to demonstrate kindness is to those who are weak within our society. Acts 20:35 says, "I have shown you in every way, by laboring like this, that you must support the weak. And remember the words of the Lord Jesus, that He said, 'It is more blessed to give than to receive." A person can be weak in a variety of ways. They may be weak socially, emotionally, materially, physically, or spiritually. In James 1:27, we read "Pure religion and undefiled before God and the Father is this, To visit the fatherless and widows in their affliction, and to keep himself unspotted from the world." Widows and orphans are often financially poor and we should look after their financial needs, of course. Notice the word used in this passage is "visit" Widows and orphans are often emotionally weak or struggling because of their state. We should also seek to be a companion and friend to them as best we can. The New International Version (NIV) uses the words "look after" instead of visit. This could simply be taking care of whatever needs a widow or orphan might have, be it financial, physical, emotional, or spiritual. Think of a widow, many are older and may require help to do certain physical tasks. They may need to mow the lawn, clean their house, or prepare meals. An orphan may need someone to take them to an activity that a dad might do like going to a game.

Of course, the context is specifically widows and orphans, but it could apply to anyone needing additional help because of their circumstances. Jesus said that those who would be welcomed into the kingdom would be those that served. Not as a matter of a work's salvation, but that as your heart is moved in love, it would cause a work in you. Mathew 25:35, 36 says, "for I was hungry and you gave Me food; I was thirsty, and you gave Me drink; I was a stranger and you took Me in; 36 I was naked and you clothed Me; I was sick and you visited Me; I was in prison and you came to Me." We know from verses later in the chapter that when you help anyone in need you are doing unto Christ. These two verses mention a variety of ways you can show kindness to others. Some have obvious material needs, such as those that are naked, hungry, or thirsty. Some have emotional needs such as the stranger, sick, or prisoner. We know with the sick that we should pray for their recovery (James 5:14-16), but we should also be willing to spend time with them, which can be just as important in showing kindness to them. It may help them recover faster as well. The stranger could be anyone that is lonely, isolated, new or ostracized by others. They may be someone that really has a rough time fitting in. This could mean just being a friend to someone who doesn't have any friends.

One group that Jesus says to go visit is those in prison. This one can be a difficult one for many. Some are in prison because they are being persecuted for Christ or have been wrongly convicted. For most, though, they are in prison for actual crimes they committed. Though difficult, we should show mercy and compassion to them as well. Let them see your Light and love, and in so doing, they might see Christ. Prisoners are often broken people who have struggled with things their whole life. Many didn't come from excellent homes. This isn't to excuse their actions, but simply a call to show compassion toward them. There's always hope, and everyone deserves love and compassion. Remember, the Apostle Paul himself was a murderer of Christians. If he can find redemption, anyone can. Paul even called himself the chief of sinners. (I Timothy 1:15). Half our New Testament and the Apostle to the nations (Gentiles) was a former murder. Think about that!

One key example of kindness and compassion shown toward someone who was weak was in the parable of the Good Samaritan. (Luke 10:25-37). In this story, Jesus tells us about a Priest who passed by a stranger who had been beaten up and robbed. The Priest noticed the stranger but failed to offer any assistance to him. A Levite came by later and also failed to help the poor stranger who was suffering. Then a Samaritan came by and put him on his donkey. He took him to town and got him a room at an inn. The Samaritan bandaged the stranger up and gave money to the Innkeeper to look after him until he could return. Samaritans were looked down upon by the Jewish people and hated. They were a half-breed that arose after Israel was scattered. They were part Jewish but also had Gentile ancestry as well. The moral of the story is to show love and kindness to all people. This was more important than your status in society. To be an "important" person in the world's eyes matters nothing to God as being considered lowly. What makes you truly a follower of God is if you show love. We need to remember this today. Don't ever become so important in your own eyes or the world's eyes that you fail to get your hands dirty and help those in need. Love was always shown first by helping the weak among us. It is the genuine test of a follower of Jesus, as we see when Jesus judges the nations in Matthew 25. Working a soup kitchen can show more godliness than being on a key board within your church or nonprofit organization. Sometimes it can be as simple as stopping the work on a big project and paying attention to your child who needs you. I speak from personal experience.

SHOW KINDNESS TO YOUR ENEMIES

Jesus took the teaching of love to another level. The Old Testament had clearly taught us to love our neighbor, but Jesus said to love our enemy as well. Mathew 5:43, 44.

> 43 "You have heard that it was said, 'You shall love your neighbor and hate your enemy.' 44 [o]But I say to you, love your enemies, bless those who curse you, do good to those who hate you, and pray for those who spitefully use you and persecute you,

Jesus first reminded them that they all heard to love their neighbor. Now He was going to expand their understanding of what love and the kindness of God truly required. This was a revolutionary teaching at the time and must have shocked many who heard it. Jesus said to show kindness to those that persecute and mistreat you. To show love to those that curse you. This probably is one of the most difficult things for a believer to do. It might be easy to give lip service and say "oh I love everyone, I even love my enemies", but can you put your money where your mouth is? Can you actually show kindness to someone when they have only shown your cruelty? When you can do this, you can truly walk as a child of the Light. If you can get to the point where you show kindness to such people, you can love anyone. Everything else is a snap compared to that.

Luke covers another aspect of this teaching in his recording of Jesus' teaching. Luke says in 6:35 "love your enemies! Do good to them. Lend to them without expecting to be repaid. Then your reward from heaven will be very great, and you will truly act as children of the Most High, for he is kind to those who are unthankful and wicked." Jesus is telling us to lend money to those that persecute us. This, again, might be a difficult teaching. I may be able to say a kind word and make a few kind gestures to a cruel person, but can I open up my wallet and actually give them money with no strings attached? Money is one of the most difficult things to give to others, even to family and friends, but now you are to give it to your enemy! One has to ask if you truly love someone. Are they really an enemy? Jesus may, in fact, be teaching us to regard no one as our enemy. They may regard you as an enemy, but you love them as a friend. You treat them as you would a close friend.

SHOW KINDNESS TO THE STRANGER

Something somewhat like loving your enemy is to love a stranger because you don't know yet whether they are a friend or foe. In Hebrews 13:2 it says, "Don't forget to show hospitality to strangers, for some who have done this have entertained angels without realizing it!" We should show hospitality or kindness to strangers that we encounter. Yes, we should show such kindness out of a heart of love and compassion, but the writer gives another interesting reason to show kindness to a stranger. What if they turn out to be an angel? I don't know how common this is, but apparently, it can happen. We know that Angels visited people throughout the Bible. One time was when Abraham entertained angels. (See Genesis 18) Why is it important to be kind to angels beyond the importance of showing kindness to everyone? I'm uncertain of the answer. Maybe angels are messengers of God directly, and to disrespect, the messenger is to disrespect the one that sent him. It may also be that angels may come with a special blessing for you.

One hot issue today is immigration. The Old Testament actually has quite a bit to say about those that immigrate to the land and how you are to treat them. They are the strangers to all. We can take these verses to also apply to the stranger next door in our own lives. In Leviticus 19:34 it says, "The stranger who dwells among you shall be to you as [a]one born among you, and you shall love him as yourself; for you were strangers in the land of Egypt: I *am* the Lord your God." You are to treat the stranger like a child born to you or as a brother or sister. They are to be family to you. In other translations, it uses the word citizens. They are not to be singled out and treated differently from those native-born or born within your house. Notice it gives a reminder of when you were strangers in Egypt. We are to treat a stranger with kindness because we were strangers to someone at some point.

You are to treat the stranger with kindness. In Ezekiel 47:22 it says, "It shall be that you will divide it by lot as an inheritance for yourselves, and for the strangers who dwell among you and who bear children among you. They shall be to you as native-born among the children of Israel; they shall have an inheritance with you among the tribes of Israel." You are to mutually share with the stranger and treat them as one of your own. This seems a far cry from what many argue today. Many want such strangers to be given nothing while a citizen gets everything. Not that you should give handouts beyond what others get, but there should be equity. This would seem in line with the idea that the United States is a nation of immigrants. Unless you are Native American, we all descend from strangers to this land.

Within the church, we are to show kindness to the stranger just as we do those within the household of God. Romans 12:13 says, "distributing to the needs of the saints, given[a] to hospitality." As we show hospitality to the stranger, it may incline them to join the household of God and become one with us in the faith. Even if they don't, however, we should continue to show compassion toward them as we are able to do so.

KINDNESS IS PART OF DISCIPLESHIP

Jesus said in Matthew 16:24, 25, "Then Jesus said to His disciples, "If anyone desires to come after Me, let him deny himself, and take up his cross, and follow Me. 25 For whoever desires to save his life will lose it, but whoever loses his life for My sake will find it." (NIV) The act of discipleship requires that we pick up our cross daily to follow Him. The cross was a form of execution that Christ would ultimately go to. A believer may end up literally dying for Christ at some point, but since it says "daily", we know it's talking in a more spiritual sense of how we are to live our lives. Remember how we saw that we are to love our enemies and show kindness to them? This requires that we release things such as anger, pride, bitterness, and allow ourselves to embrace something far better, which is agape love. We may also have to do this with those we love. Just let go of the need to be right. The need to win the fight and always get the last word in. I've found that simply letting go and showing kindness and compassion is far better than pushing to show how I'm right or how I am the victim. The level of peace that you get from releasing such things is incredible. I've found that even if you prove your rightness with the ones you love, you usually do so at a significant cost that at the end of the day is never worth it. There is something profound in releasing all the negativity in our life. Jesus gave us the pattern by letting go of his dominion to come to earth and die for us. This is a good thing to meditate on, releasing all negative emotions to God. It is cathartic, to say the least, and can transform your life.

The death is to self, which is our own selfishness or what some call the ego. The ego wants its own way. It's greedy, lustful, prideful, hateful, and ultimately fearful. This is why generosity is so important. You want to become selfless rather than selfish. Like, being kind to those who upset or hurt us, we find that generosity toward others brings the true peace and happiness we all want. This is why Jesus said, "it's better to give than receive". (Acts 20:35) The blessing is both emotional and spiritual, which is far better than anything financial we may give up in the process. There are times, we may receive a financial blessing down the road as well, but that will pale in comparison to the spiritual and emotional blessings. Again, release the need to hold on to your wealth so tightly. Let the need for security and my own way go, and see what God will do in your life. You truly do find life by letting go, not holding on. You find a life actually worth living and one that you know deep down you were intended to live. You become an authentic child of the Light.

The first step to discipleship is to give back. This is what John Stange shared with me on one of my podcasts. This is what He does within his own discipleship program.[20] Give of yourself, and you begin to release the selfishness we all have. Many have found that when people are suffering emotionally, the best therapy is simply going out and helping others. As you help others heal and have their needs met, you allow yourself to heal. Remember, I had talked about the importance of loving yourself and caring for yourself? This is absolutely true, but one key way you can do this is by showing kindness and compassion to others. It's a paradox, but also part of the connection that we all have as human beings. We do have a oneness. If you harm others, you invite harm back to you. If you show kindness to others, it invites kindness back to you. This is how the golden rule works in a full circle.

KINDNESS IS AN ACT OF LIBERATION

We've had many "liberation movements" over the years, but the greatest liberation movement is to live out love and kindness. Think of those that are or were oppressed and mistreated. Whether it's women, minorities, immigrants, etc., all would truly be liberated if they were treated with kindness. In kindness, there can be nothing less than equality and dignity. Love demands true respect. You can't show compassion without recognizing every individual is worthy of dignity. There is no room for any mistreatment.

The gospel brings freedom to those that embrace it, and so too is it with kindness. In Isaiah 61:1, it says "The Spirit of the Lord God *is* upon Me Because the Lord has anointed Me To preach good tidings to the poor; He has sent Me to [a]heal the brokenhearted, To proclaim liberty to the captives, And the opening of the prison to *those who are* bound;" When we bring kindness to others, we have a way of liberating them.

The prisons people are in are rarely literal, but emotional and spiritual. When people are shown kindness, it can break the chains of depression, stress, anxiety, and fear. This is also true for those showing the kindness. You can help to break the chains of stress and depression in your life. You can walk with a new purpose in your life. Kindness has a way of changing our perspective on life and puts us into a different state of mind.

We all have heard John 8:32 which says "you shall know the truth, and the truth shall make you free.". What is the greatest truth out there? Love. Some would say God, but remember, God is love. Kindness is love in action. So living in kindness is to actively live in truth. When we live contrary to love and kindness, regardless of what form that might take, we really are living out a lie. Fear, hatred, anger, and cruelty are all falsehoods that people practice. When you live in falsehoods, you aren't free, you're putting yourself in bondage. You imprison your mind and soul in a dark cell. You can't live out your true identity and be liberated without love and kindness. Choose to be authentic this day and practice the truth with kindness!

KINDNESS WITHIN THE HOUSEHOLD OF GOD

We are to show kindness to everyone, including the stranger, just as we would those within the household of God. There seems to be a priority given to those within the faith. Galatians 6:10 says, "Therefore, as we have the opportunity, let us do good to all, especially to those who are of the household of faith." Notice that it says to do good to all, no one should be excluded from our kindness and love. The priority exists within the church because we are a family. Most would understand that your first priority is always your family. You have a literal family, then you have your church family. You might even break it down within the family in terms of priority. You have a greater duty to those within your immediate family than to those more distant relatives. The same would be true within the church. We would have a duty first within our own congregation, then to other believers in other churches.

We are commanded to love everyone, which includes neighbor and enemy alike, but Jesus gave a specific command of love for those within the faith. John 13:35 says, "By this, all will know that you are My disciples, if you have love for one another." Love, in general, sends the message that we are followers of Christ, but love for one another specifically shows that we are his disciples and patterning our life on Him.

KINDNESS TOWARD OTHERS IS KINDNESS TO JESUS

Mathew 25:34-40, Proverbs 19:17, Hebrews 13:1-3

We are familiar with this passage in Matthew 25:37-40 which says,

> 37 "Then the righteous will answer Him, saying, 'Lord, when did we see You hungry and feed *You,* or thirsty and give *You* drink? 38 When did we see You a stranger and take *You* in, or naked and clothe *You?* 39 Or when did we see You sick, or in prison, and come to You?' 40 And the King will answer and say to them, 'Assuredly, I say to you, inasmuch as you did *it* to one of the least of these My brethren, you did *it* to Me.'

This is a beautiful sentiment, and we totally believe it to be true? What does this really mean, though? In one sense, it is true in that Jesus greatly cares for humanity and particularly those that are poor and suffering. We have a concept in our society that seems to have caught on a few years ago, though I think the concept goes back much further. I'm speaking of the concept of paying it forward. Someone does something kind for you, and then you commit to doing something kind for something else in the future. Someone may have given you some money that you desperately needed when you were broke to buy groceries, so you do the same years later for someone else who is in need like you once were. We do as Christians seek to pay it forward toward others because of the love Jesus did for us, and how He has blessed us. There's much more than that going on in the teachings of this passage, however.

The Bible teaches the concept of the family of man. That we all came from a common source. (See Acts 17). So, in a sense, we show kindness to Christ and God by showing kindness to others. Much like you show kindness to your parents by being kind towards your siblings. Again, this is all true, but the spiritual truth of this passage goes deeper. Since Jesus Himself came down as a man, He became part of the human family and has that direct connection with us all.

We have a spiritual family of believers, which is referenced throughout scripture. We are the children of God, not just in a literal creational sense, but also in a spiritual sense by faith. We are brothers and sisters to each other. This creates an even deeper oneness than the family of man in creation. This too captures an aspect of truth in the passage above, because He specifically references the brethren. There's a special call to help fellow believers. This does connect us to Christ. Jesus in the spiritual family is our elder brother.

The church is also pictured as the body of Christ. (See Romans 12:5,1, Colossians 1:18, and Ephesians 3:6). In this spiritual picture, to look after others within the body is to care for Christ Himself. If a part of the body was broken and we mended it, it's as if we mended the arm of Jesus. When looked at this way, the passage takes on a more profound meaning.

The church is also the bride of Christ, so when we care for those that have needs within the church, we care for Christ's bride. This is quite a touching thought. Would you feel more endeared to someone who showed love and compassion toward your wife when she was in need?

I think there may also be a connection to Christ in helping others in that we also share in his divinity. Call it whatever you like, being in the image of God, holding the spark of divinity within you, we all share his divine imprint within us. So like a spiritually unified body, this divine body of oneness is also real.

This may make some feel a bit uncomfortable, but at least if you can see that every human being is an image-bearer of God, start with that.

We had mentioned that our actions are like a ripple in the water. An act of kindness that we do for others keeps going out. This is true even without a direct commitment to pay it forward because it's a cosmic law. It has a way of circling back to us as well. Kinda like those long circular stacks of dominoes. One starts it all off and quickly it spreads and goes back to the original source. We should keep the circle going. Christ pushed the first domino down, let us fall in line so to speak, and love others as it works it back to Him.

Remember, we had discussed the cosmic bank account for sin? There's a bank account for kindness too, not to save us, but to bless us. Christ already paid for sin at the cross. This idea goes back to the Old Testament as it says in Proverbs 19:17 "He who has pity on the poor lends to the Lord, And He will pay back what he has given."

THE CONNECTION BETWEEN KINDNESS AND WISDOM

There is a definite correlation between wisdom and kindness. Solomon recognized it when speaking of the virtuous woman. Proverbs 31:26 says, "She opens her mouth with wisdom, And on her tongue *is* the law of kindness." Kindness is a key to possessing wisdom. Have you ever noticed that kind people tend to possess deep wisdom? Whether in our personal lives or those we admire from history. Wisdom is not the same as knowledge or intelligence. You can have a great deal of knowledge, but not be wise. You can also be wise and not necessarily be learned. Wisdom goes to the issue of prudence. A wise person can easily recognize that cruelty, nastiness, and selfishness doesn't really serve them. They are kind because they love others, but they also know that being unkind will not bring the peace and happiness

I desire for my own life. People may think being unkind will get them ahead, but will it really be for the long haul? Will you find satisfaction and contentment in it? If you look deep within your heart, you know the answer is no. Kindness brings greater joy and fulfillment in life because we are living more authentically as human beings. We are living more as God intended for us to live. It reflects who He is in his nature.

I've heard of a rule called enlightened self-interest from several sources over the years. It basically says that it's in your own best interest to look out for others and not just yourself. Kindness has a way of coming back to you, as we have said earlier. Paul said in Galatians 6:7 "Do not be deceived, God is not mocked; for whatever a man sows, that he will also reap." We will get back what we put out. Sometimes the principle of reaping and sowing is called "karma" in today's world, but the concept, as people use the term, commonly is the same. If you want kindness to be shown to you, show kindness. This is a general rule, of course. There may be times you show kindness, and it's not met with kindness, but generally, it is. Also, it's important to recognize that its kindness showed over time. You can't show kindness once and expect a bounty of kindness immediately. You may get a special blessing from one act of kindness, but like seeds, it needs to be cultivated and allowed to grow over time. The wise person understands this. For with kindness, patience is also necessary.

Application

1. Think of 3 acts of kindness you have shown to others in your life. It doesn't matter if they were big or small. How did it make you feel? What can you have done to have shown even more kindness in those moments, if anything? What now can you do to show similar kindness to others? Write down your responses in your journal.

2. Write down 3 instances where you did not show kindness in your life. They can be big or small? What could you have done

differently?

3. Write down 3 acts of kindness shown to you. Can you do an act of kindness for someone else that is similar to those acts?

7. LET JUDGMENTS GO

"Judge[a] not, that you be not judged. 2 For with what [b]judgment you judge, you will be judged; and with the measure you use, it will be measured back to you." (Mathew 7:1,2)

When people read the above passage about not judging others, there seems to be two extremes that we can fall into. The first one is basically to ignore everything. It's as if we pretend that there's no such thing as right or wrong. We become like the three monkeys covering our eyes, ears, and mouth. See no evil, hear no evil, speak no evil. This is not a realistic approach to this verse or to life itself. If you see someone about to kill or seriously injure someone else, you would hopefully step in and try to protect the innocent person. You, in that moment, make a snap judgment about the situation and persons involved and take action.

There's a second extreme that some fall into with this verse. They completely render it meaningless, possibly even teaching that the passage says we should in fact judge, which contradicts the verse on its face. How are we to make sense of this verse in the real world without simply discarding it? This is a key question if we are to walk in the Light.

HAVE NO CONDEMNATION IN YOUR JUDGMENTS

We have clear values taught in scripture. We know things like adultery, drunkenness, stealing, etc. are wrong. When you see someone doing something like this, it's obvious they are violating what is right. How do you respond in such a situation? Paul in Romans 1 went through a whole litany of sins that were being committed in Rome and Corinth, as well as the Roman world in general. He lays out the sins in detail. Yet, we get to chapter 2, and Paul says this in verse 1, "Therefore you are inexcusable, O man, whoever you are who judge, for in whatever you judge another you condemn yourself; for you who judge practice the same things." He has just laid out the sins of Rome, yet He tells us plainly not to judge. Why are we not to judge those in sin? The answer is given simply that we do or have done the same things. Paul is saying we condemn ourselves when we judge them. The idea here is not to turn a blind eye to the obvious. The point of not judging them is that you don't condemn them. Refrain from the finger waving and shame. Reframe from the nasty thoughts, "oh that disgusting vile person, how can they do that". If you condemn them, you open yourself up to the same condemnation. It doesn't mean you can't see and access the obvious. It doesn't mean you can't try to help them to move in a better direction if possible. You want to approach everyone with grace, love, compassion, and understanding. You want to maybe understand why they may be doing what they're doing. This will help to build greater empathy and compassion. You also want to always be aware of where you may be doing or have done similar things in your own life. Even if not outwardly, within your heart, you may have done the same things.

The word Jesus and Paul use for judge is krinō, which means "to separate, put asunder, to pick out, select, choose to approve, esteem" It also carries with it the idea of setting forth a decree.[21] It's basically like you're the Judge in the courtroom pronouncing a judgment on someone. This goes along with the concept of condemnation because only a judge can do this and then pronounce a sentence. This also goes along with Jesus' teaching on pulling the plank out of your bother's eye when you have a whole wood board in yours. We aren't even qualified to sit in judgment of others. When we look at other people, we need to take off the Judge's robe and lay down the gavel. We are to be more like a teacher and physician. Helping people to heal and move forward is what we do. We want to help people move into the Light along with us if they are willing and ready to do so. If they aren't, we seek to show love and set an example for them. When you take on the role of teacher and healer, you can also teach yourself at the same time. A judge sitting in judgment never does this. We're not the judge or cop seeking to be the faultfinder, but a servant that is to point people upward.

Jesus taught us to call no one a fool. Mathew 5:22, says, "But I say to you that whoever is angry with his brother [e]without a cause shall be in danger of the judgment. And whoever says to his brother, 'Raca!'[f] shall be in danger of the council. But whoever says, [g]'You fool!' shall be in danger of [h]hell fire." One thing I had wondered about was what Raca meant. I looked at the Strong's Concordance and found it means empty-headed or a person lacking sense. It was a common term in Jesus' day. It's roughly the equivalent of calling someone an idiot today. Doesn't fool mean basically the same thing? A fool does refer to someone lacking sense or not too bright. Fool also refers to someone lacking wisdom. The two are similar. I think the difference is a matter of degree. Fool is a stronger word than Raca. It might be the difference between idiot and moron. I had always thought of being called a moron was worse than being called an idiot. To demean someone or speak condescendingly to a person by name-calling is seen as worse than being angry without cause in our original verse. We should seek to always speak and think of others with dignity and respect. The context isn't limited to calling someone a fool, but any type of demeaning words directed at another person. Some today find it funny to refer to others as "dumbasses", (we will assume they mean dumb donkeys). We should not even take amusement in the demeaning of others, even if we are not the ones making the comment. To take pleasure in the degrading of others is just as bad as doing the degrading ourselves.

Many have tried to undercut this verse and not make about what it says on its face. Some have said that Jesus called people fools. The closest to this is Mathew 23:17, 19. Go back to verse 16 to get the context. It says, "Woe to you, blind guides, who say, 'Whoever swears by the temple, it is nothing; but whoever swears by the gold of the temple, he is obliged *to perform it.*' The context is a category of people who would profess to be guides to the people. Verse 17 says "Fools and blind! For which is greater, the gold or the temple that [i]sanctifies the gold? Then verse 19 says, "Fools and blind! For which is greater, the gift or the altar that sanctifies the gift? "Notice that in neither verse does Jesus ever call a specific person a fool directly? He never personally attacked anyone by calling them a fool. When you consider the context, he is saying to do such things as elevate gold or gifts above God is a foolish thing to do. He does in some of his parables refer to foolish behaviors and may reference a person in the story as a fool, but it's always within the context of teaching a point and never a personal attack on an actual person.

CORPORATE JUDGMENT WITHIN THE CHURCH

There is a time for judgment much like a judge in a courtroom would make, but this is within the church and would be a corporate judgment. In Matthew 18:15-18 and I Corinthians, we get the process and reasons when this happens. Jesus speaks of when a brother or sister sins against you, that you first go to them and seek to work it out with them and quickly reconcile, if possible. If they will not listen, then go with two or three others to confront them. If they still will not listen, then you take it before the church. Notice it says "sin against". The offending party is causing harm to you or someone else. This isn't a witch-hunt for all possible sins in their life. You have a recognized victim.

Now, Paul extends it for the overall protection of the church and to protect the witness of Christ in I Corinthians. In the specific case Paul references, it was a young man who was committing adultery with his father's wife, i.e. his stepmother. So you had the witness of Christ being harmed. He says this sin isn't even common among the world outside the church. You may also have the father as a victim as well. We aren't sure if he is living or not. It includes an element of incest on top of adultery. It's critical to see that the level needs to be causing harm to another or be of such a public nature and severity so as to cause harm to the name of Christ. So often, some churches will discipline any sin they disapprove of or alleged sin they don't like. I remember being in a church where a person was confronted about going to a bar, which is questionable where that is even a sin, let alone a sin worthy of church discipline. Now, alcoholism would be a different story.

The discipline given for grave sin is limiting contact with the person until they repent. This can include disfellowshipping. The contact listed was eating with them, which was an intimate activity in this culture. Don't have intimate associations with them while under discipline. This discipline is to get them to repent and change course. It also promotes reconciliation once this has happened. Once the person has repented, the discipline is to end. There is not to be additional "punishment" as some type of retribution or to rub it in their face. Again, I've heard of churches putting time parameters on the disfellowshipping for six months. If the person repents tomorrow, then they should be brought back in. No further discipline should continue.

This is a tough-love approach that the church takes as a last resort. The church only has jurisdiction within the church, i.e. people outside the church cannot fall under church discipline. I believe there are situations where an individual may need to separate or limit contact with another person as well. If you have a family member who is abusive or an addict, you may need to cut them off for a period of time if they will not seek help. This would obviously include a spouse that abused the other spouse or the children. You might need to cut off a spouse or adult child who is an alcoholic or drug addict until they seek help. If a spouse is unfaithful and will not stop, you may need to separate there as well. Like with the church, the goal should be reconciliation with them once repentance occurs. Part of the reason you may need to separate may be to protect yourself and others. Another reason may be that you're not enabling the behavior.

What should the attitude be when a church disciplines? It should be one of love and compassion. Members should refrain from gossiping, backbiting, or speaking negatively of the person. There should be no hatred, bitterness, disparaging, or nastiness expressed about or toward the person. This should be a somber moment that deeply pains the church.

JUDGING OURSELVES

Our judgments of ourselves are often the harshest. We are our own worst critics. We condemn ourselves by belittling, degrading, and constantly criticizing ourselves. Sometimes we will use name-calling in our own minds. These judgments speak condemnation to our souls. They keep us from going forward. What we need to do is let go of these judgments about ourselves. When you make a mistake or see faults in your own life. Give yourself some grace. Approach yourself with love and kindness, just as you should others. You need a break as much as anyone else in this world, and you have no more right to put yourself down than anyone else. When you put yourself down, you speak ill of who you are in Christ. You also make it more difficult to be the genuine servant of Christ that can walk as a child of the Light.

Recall how we had said, your focus should be on love rather than sin? That this is how you truly grow? Well, you need to take time to meditate on love, which includes for yourself. You need to meditate on becoming all that God has for you. Dwelling on judgments and criticisms of yourself is counterproductive. Pray to fully manifest the fruits of the Spirit. Quickly ask God to wash your sins away but never wallow in those sins as you pray. Don't hide in shame, but proclaim who you are in Christ and who you are becoming in Him.

JUDGMENTS WEIGH US AND OTHERS DOWN

Have you ever noticed one common element among people who are stressed, depressed, or just unhappy? What do they all tend to do a lot of? They all make a lot of judgments. They are constantly expressing judgments about others, themselves, or the situations or circumstances they're in. You can almost guarantee that they are making even more internal judgments that they may not be expressing verbally. Think of times in your own life when you were depressed or unhappy. Were you making a lot of judgments in those moments? My guess is that you were.

When we express a lot of judgment, we take ourselves into a dark, negative place. We are helping to poison our souls with negative judgmental emotions. How can you fully walk in the Light if you are going down dark pathways in your mind? These judgments can even start to affect your health. So much unnecessary illness is brought on by our judgments as we focus on them day in and day out.

I think maybe part of the judgment Christ was speaking of when He said "judge not lest you be judged" is when we judge ourselves. Yes, it's speaking of the judgment of others which may bring the judgment of God on us, but could it also be speaking of the judgment of ourselves as well? As you judge others, you start judging yourself more. As you feed judgments about yourself, you often multiply those judgments because you are now creating a mindset that goes in a direction of judgment. You start to operate out of a reactive, judgmental mind. I speak from experience with this. We are a product of our thoughts, and they create a perception of how we view ourselves and the world around us.

Most reading this book have strong values and beliefs, which is good. One problem we can fall into is judging ourselves when we don't fully live up to them. None of us completely walks out what we believe. We can start to wallow about how we come up short. These constant judgments, however, don't actually tend to help us. Yes, occasionally you can change through shame and move forward. My experience is, though, it can only take you so far. What actually works better than beating ourselves up is to show love, compassion, and empathy toward ourselves. I see more alignment with my values by doing this. We can say the same for how we speak to others. You may be able to shame a person to change to some extent, but you're likely to help them positively change more by showing them love, kindness, and compassion.

JUDGMENTS OFTEN COME FROM A FEELING OF LACK

I love this from Gabrielle Bernstein, who wrote in her book Judgment Detox, "The root cause of all judgment is the fear of not being good enough, not being worthy of love, and not being safe."[22] I think there is so much truth in the statement. With judgments of others and even to ourselves, we are hiding our own fear and insecurity. We don't feel good enough within our own souls. Sometimes we can see this in a child. The child defects in his or her own shortcomings by attempting to point out what someone else did that was the "real" reason why they did what they did or why something went wrong. Whether or not the statement makes any sense, we easily see through it as an excuse. The question is, why can't we see our own judgments as often being the same thing as what the child is doing? It might be better to dress it up. We may make it sound more articulate and "reasonable" sounding, but it remains an excuse. We are simply hiding behind the judgment. What if we didn't need to create the excuse in the first place? What if we dropped the judgment of ourselves and others because we knew we were truly worthy of love, compassion, and goodness?

Once you start to understand the nature of God's unconditional love, it may be easier to let go of such judgments. It may be that we have this or that in our life, but God loves us anyway, so drop the judgment and criticism of ourselves. Maybe this person did this or that, or has this issue in their life, but again, recognize that God loves that person unconditionally exactly where they are in this moment. God will love you and that other person regardless of whether or not change occurs. Yes, we always pray and hope for positive change. We all want to see that happen, but we can release the judgments and embrace the love for them and ourselves, regardless.

If you can stop and recognize that your judgments are most likely coming from a place of feeling unworthy or unlovable, then you can start to affirm the truth about yourself. You can start to meditate on the fact that you are worthy of all good things, which include love and kindness. You can find security because you can do anything through God's help as it says in Philippians 4:13, "I can do all things through [a]Christ who strengthens me." I often use this verse as one of my affirmations in the morning and at night. It's a great verse to take into your meditation times as well.

THE ACCEPTANCE OF ALL THINGS

Once you release all judgments about yourself, others, and situations. The next step is to accept all things as they are. You want to let go of all negative emotions such as anger, frustration, fear, and hostility go. Whether those feelings about yourself or others. It may also be about circumstances that you have no control over or limited control at best. Let go of the need to fix the situation or person.

Allow yourself to be at complete peace. Turn over everything to God, which makes acceptance of where you are right now much easier. You can pray about God helping you to accept all things. Recognize that God is in control of all things. His hand of the provision will be upon you. You can also begin to accept things as they are within your meditation. Commit to and embrace this acceptance in prayer and meditation. Leave the baggage at the door of your life.

Just like with letting judgments go, this is not about making excuses for wrong actions in others or yourself. It's also not about becoming complacent. It's about yielding all things to his Spirit. There's great liberation and freedom in simply letting go of the frustration and struggle and embracing where you are in this moment.

Remember, too, that life is a journey. We are all on that journey and we are all at different levels in our lives. Our paths take different turns and twists that are unique to us. Allow yourself to enjoy the journey. All and respect the journey that others are taking. We sometimes want to help people along their journey to make better choices. We want to save them some heartache. This is good and commendable. But allow them the freedom ultimately to make their own choices without judgment or condemnation. Love them and be there for them even when you can see they are going down a dark road, and you've warned them about it. Be there for them when they see the errors and help them get back on track if they are amenable to that.

We always, with acceptance, want to be there with compassion, understanding, and empathy. This includes not only other people but ourselves. Often I look back at my life and can see so many choices that were not so great. I went down some dark paths myself. I have just learned to accept that it was part of my journey. I understand that it was all a learning and growing experience. When I reflect on them, I want to show myself love and kindness. I believe this is God's perspective. If you have adult children, do you still harbor anger or resentment about a tantrum they threw when they were 3 years old? Do you still hold bitterness when they were disobedient at that age now? I'm guessing for most reading this, they have long moved on. This gives a picture of God to a certain extent. He's not holding anger or resentment for something you did 30 years ago. In all honesty, he didn't have any when you committed the act or thought back then, but like a human parent, certainly not today.

Once you can accept things as they are, you can then more fully want in his Light. You can now truly move forward. I think this may be why so many recovery programs have acceptance as a part of their program. It's a cathartic experience and the only way to truly make a transformation. We may not be alcoholics or drug addicts, but it's a good thing for all people to do. We all have shortcomings and the world is far from perfect, but once you accept it, you're in a place to go forward as a child of the Light.

Application

1. Consciously choose to let all judgments of yourself and others go. Release all bitterness, anger, criticism, and resentment. You can do this right now, but choose to release it. Pray to God and release it to Him.

2. In your meditation, specifically focus on letting on judgments go. Visualize them being released from within you. Accept all things as they are in this moment and praise God within your meditation for where He has you in this moment.

8. KNOW WHO YOU ARE!

"as His divine power has given to us all things that pertain to life and godliness, through the knowledge of Him who called us by glory and virtue, by which have been given to us exceedingly great and precious promises, that through these you may be partakers of the divine nature, having escaped the [c]corruption that is in the world through lust." (II Peter 1:3,4)

One of the most important things to walking as a child of the Light is to know who you are and what you have in Him spiritually. Knowing it intellectually is only a small part of it, though. You must embrace it within your being. It has to be something you know within your heart. Once you begin to walk in your true reality, much of the struggle ceases to be in your life. You stop trying to be something or become something in Him. You realize you already are all that you need to be within yourself by His power. It's only a matter of manifesting it and walking it out. This is where sanctification happens, but there really is no time frame for it. You could become fully realized in Him instantly.

Yes, we do have things that pull us away, and we doubt ourselves, but the truth of our being remains. For much of our lives, even our Christian lives, we live under the illusion that we are weak and need something more. This really is a false identity that we often live under. We need to start walking in our true reality. Have I fully thrown off this erroneous identity? No, even now I still struggle with it, but over the past few years, I've moved much closer to my true identity. I am starting to more fully embrace who I am and it's wonderful! Don't expect that you will fully walk in it overnight, but believe who you are right now. Let that knowledge grow within you.

YOU ARE THE VERY IMAGE OF GOD

We were made in the very image of God. Genesis 1:27 says, "So God created man in His own image; in the image of God He created him; male and female He created them." What does being in the image of God mean? One aspect is that we reflect the nature of God. We have intellect, emotions, ethics, creativity, and self-awareness. Animals may possess some of these qualities, but even where they possess a quality, they tend not to have it to the same extent that humans do. Self-awareness is probably the vast gulf between humans and most animals. There may be a few animals that possess a rudimentary understanding of self, but it would pale in comparison to that of humans. Most animals, when they see themselves in the mirror, have no awareness that it is a reflection of themselves. They generally think it's another animal. Being aware of yourself in a mirror is only a tiny portion of self-awareness, though. We've never observed an animal contemplating philosophy or engaging in deep introspection. I do find it interesting that a gorilla named Koko was able to be taught sign language, which does point to a level of abstract thought. She was limited in how far she could go with it, much like a young child in understanding.

Being in the image of God also puts a divine imprint on us. A spark of divinity, you might say. Some are extremely uncomfortable with this idea, but a special touch of the creator was placed on us. Genesis 2:7 says, "And the Lord God formed man of the dust of the ground, and breathed into his nostrils the breath of life, and man became a living being." (KJV) I believe animals have a soul as well, but they were not imparted with a special breath or touch of God as humans were from the beginning. I like to think of God as the ocean and we are a drop from that ocean.

Jesus actually referred to our divine aspect when He said in John 10:34, "Jesus answered them, Is it not written in your law, I said, Ye are gods?" Jesus was quoting from Psalms 82:6. Many have pointed out that it was a reference to men being judges and rulers in Psalms. This is true, but within the context of John 10, Jesus was quoting it to defend his own deity as the Son of God. He's actually defending his deity by referencing our divinity clearly. To limit it to men being judges in that context would make no sense. It would be saying "I'm the Son of God but you're judges", it would be like "yeah so, what does that have to do with your claim to being deity?" I don't believe He is saying we are gods in a separate sense from God. There is only one God. He is pointing to our divinity in God, though.

We have an eternal aspect of our beings. Not just in the sense that we will live forever, but that we have existed in God for all eternity. God said to the Prophet in Jeremiah 1:5, "Before I formed you in the womb I knew you; Before you were born I sanctified[a] you; I [b]ordained you a prophet to the nations." Notice it doesn't say I knew you would come, or even that I ordained that you would come. It says I knew you, present tense. This knowing was relational, and that we existed to God already. So when God made man, that eternal piece of God was imprinted.

We are not just the spiritual children of God, but all humans are the literal children of God as well. Acts 17:29 says, "Therefore since we are the offspring of God, we ought not to think that the Divine Nature is like gold or silver or stone, something shaped by art and man's devising." There is a special adoption that takes place that makes us spiritually the children of God, but all people, by creation, are God's children. If we are his children, we are the same likeness and essence as Him. Just like that drop of water from the ocean, it possesses all the basic elements of the body of water that the ocean is.

Once you realize you are a spark of divinity, everything changes in terms of how you perceive yourself and relate to others. It affects how you view others as well. If I have divinity in me, then, like God, love is my true essence. I may sin, but my true identity is not sin but love. My identity is everything connected to love, such as peace, joy, kindness, etc. This is true for every other person on the face of this planet. How can anyone not have profound dignity and value then? How can we degrade ourselves or anyone else ever again? How can we ever feel unworthy or that we aren't good enough to come to God? No person is a "loser" ever. We all have the potential to be so much more than we are right now. We have a destiny to fulfill, all of us! This puts walking as a child of Light into perspective.

WE ARE PARTAKERS OF HIS DIVINE NATURE

Remember our verse in II Peter 1:2-4 which say "as His divine power has given to us all things that pertain to life and godliness, through the knowledge of Him who called us by glory and virtue, by which have been given to us exceedingly great and precious promises, that through these you may be partakers of the divine nature, having escaped the [c]orruption that is in the world through lust." (II Peter 1:3,4) God has given us his power so that we can do all things in this world to walk in his Light. We get to tap into his divine nature. As we said above, we already have the imprint which gives us so much, but now we can tap into the source. It's kind of like our computers today. We can do so much with them, and they have a lot of storage capacity within them. Now, we have access to the spiritual internet, which is God, which gives us the power to tap into everything. We have tons more information and programming available to us than just what may be on our own computers. We can download programs too. God can be like our cloud and allow us to store more information for later than our computer itself would ever hold. We go from having a lot with our computers to now being limitless with God as our internet so to speak.

Our ability to walk as children of the Light because of God's power source greatly expands what we already were given. There're literally no obstacles that can stand in God's way, so with God, all things become possible.

Again, though, if we didn't have a degree of divinity already, how could we access all that God is within us? You have to have a computer powerful enough to access the internet. I can remember in the 1990s, you had to have a certain level of capability within your computer to even go on the internet. Older computers couldn't do this. This points to what we said before about us having the imprint of God on us. Our systems are capable of tapping into God's power. When we become a believer, God may have to clean out some programs and take some spiritual viruses off to get us up and running, but he's made our systems good enough to access Him. I believe He can give upgrades to our systems as well, though.

WE ARE GOD'S WORKMANSHIP

We are the product of God's handiwork. As it says in Ephesians 2:10, "For we are His workmanship, created in Christ Jesus for good works, which God prepared beforehand that we should walk in them." God describes Himself as the potter in Romans 9. So we are like the beautiful pottery pieces that he has made. Maybe you are like a marvelous vase. We could also think of Him as a woodcutter that carves beautiful pieces of art like doves or dolphins. The workmanship can not only be things of beauty but functional things as well, such as tools and utensils. Really, we are both beautiful and functional. Because God has carved and perfected what we are, we can know that we have everything we need to walk as a child of the Light.

Have you ever created something yourself? Have you ever created a painting or sculpture or carved something from wood that you were especially proud of? If you did, you probably felt a lot of love for that thing, because much love went into creating it. This is how God feels about us. As for his workmanship, he takes a great deal of pride in what he has done, and he loves the product he has created.

What kind of care went into us when God created us? Psalms 139:13, 14 says, "For You formed my inward parts; You [a]covered me in my mother's womb.**14** I will praise You, for [b]I am fearfully *and* wonderfully made Marvelous are Your works, And *that* my soul knows very well." We were fearfully made and wonderfully created by God. What does it mean to be fearfully made? God wasn't afraid when He made us. The word for fear could be translated reverently made. Much like when He talks about us fearing Him, we are to revere God. So it was in all reverence that He made us. It would be like if you were going to make a beautiful painting for a king, you would do so with great reverence and be meticulous in your work. God wasn't creating his work for another king, but for Himself as the king. He wanted a work that would show forth his dignity and greatness. Something worthy of his name and stature. This is who we are. We can take pride in the fact of what God made in us. This really is showing pride in God's work, of course, not our own.

How fantastic is it to realize that we are such a fine piece of God's artwork and also so well-made? This should make your heart leap for joy! You could say, I'm like God's Ferrari, so fine-tuned and powerful, yet beautiful and majestic. Just like my creator! God recognized how awesome I was and said that it was "wonderful" specifically. God created something that was a masterpiece and He recognized his greatness in it! As it says in Genesis 1:31, "Then God saw everything that He had made, and indeed *it was* very good…" We are "very good" according to God. This was right after he created humans, male and female, that he said this.

WE ARE THE TEMPLES OF GOD

If you've been a believer for any time, you have probably

heard that your body is the temple of God. I Corinthians 3:16, says, "Do you not know that you are the temple of God and *that* the Spirit of God dwells in you?" What does it mean to be the temple of God? It means that our body is the home that the Holy Spirit lives in. You might say Jesus does literally live within your heart. To be the temple of God is to be a sacred and holy place, as was the physical temple in scripture that the Jews worshiped God in. We all know this includes not polluting our bodies. Within I Corinthians, the specific context was referencing fornication, uniting our bodies with a prostitute. The context could include anything that pollutes, however, such as with smoking, drugs, or excessive alcohol. Anything that can destroy our body could apply.

It could also be used to support being a good steward of our bodies and seeking to maintain good health within it. As the temple of God, it means that the ultimate ownership of our bodies belongs to God, which should affect all that we do in and with it. A few chapters later, Paul says in I Corinthians 6:19, 20 "**19** Or do you not know that your body is the temple of the Holy Spirit *who is* in you, whom you have from God, and you are not your own? **20** For you were bought at a price; therefore, glorify God in your body [a]and in your spirit, which is God's." We own our bodies, but you might think of it as a mortgage on the house. You own it, but God is the bank holding the note.

Besides being a holy and sacred place, what type of things went on in the temple? One key thing was the sacrifices. We should be willing to make sacrifices with our time, talents, and resources in using our bodies to serve God. In Romans 12:1, it says, "I beseech[a] you therefore, brethren, by the mercies of God, that you present your bodies a living sacrifice, holy, acceptable to God, *which is* your [b]reasonable service." Part of our sacrifice is to be holy, so all unholy things should be released. A closely connected concept to release the things of the world. In the next verse, it says, "And do not be conformed to this world, but be transformed by the renewing of your mind, that you may prove what *is* that good and acceptable and perfect will of God." We will do what is acceptable to God when we renew our minds daily. We have mentioned how this is done throughout this book. Prayer, meditation, and scripture are the principal ways we can do this. Our temple is a holy thing that we should consecrate daily to God.

The power and presence are also present in our temples. All things are possible because of the spiritual presence of God. The temple of the body is superior to the physical temple. Acts 17:24 says, "God, who made the world and everything in it, since He is Lord of heaven and earth, does not dwell in temples made with hands." God had promised in the Old Testament to put the Spirit into us, as it says in Ezekiel 36:27, "I will put My Spirit within you and cause you to walk in My statutes, and you will keep My judgments and do them." Notice it will cause you to walk in God's statutes or laws. This includes the law of love itself. This same Spirit is the one who raised Jesus from the dead, so He comes with power. Romans 8:11 declares, "But if the Spirit of Him who raised Jesus from the dead dwells in you, He who raised Christ from the dead will also give life to your mortal bodies [d]through His Spirit who dwells in you.." John 16:13 tells us that the Spirit will guide us in all truth. ".However, when He, the Spirit of truth, has come, He will guide you into all truth; for He will not speak on His own *authority,* but whatever He hears, He will speak; and He will tell you things to come." The Spirit will give you the power to walk as a child of the Light as He dwells within the temple of your being.

WE ARE THE LIGHT

In the first chapter, we discussed how we are the Light of the world along with God and Christ. This is taught in Matthew 5:14:16 "

> **14** "You are the light of the world. A city that is set on a hill cannot be hidden. **15** Nor do they light a lamp and put it under a basket, but on a lampstand, and it gives light to all *who are* in the house. **16** Let your light

so shine before men, that they may see your good works and glorify your Father in heaven.

Being the Light now only makes being a witness for Him possible, as we have mentioned, but it gives us the power with which to walk in as a child of God. We walk in the exact same Light as God. We are in God's Lights, but we are also part of that Light itself. The Light within gives us all power in heaven to live a godly life. We have the same Light that Christ walked in as well. As children of the Light, always seek to walk in love, peace, and joy. In this, people will want the same thing. Our Light is not something we exclusively have but is available to anyone and everyone who will embrace his Light first. You will awaken to the Light within you as you embrace his Light.

WE ARE THE CHILDREN OF GOD

We know we are all children of God in a creational sense, but there is also a spiritual rebirth that takes place that allows us to become the spiritual children of God. This is by adoption and is really an embracing of it. We have to consciously choose to be a spiritual child of God. By simply believing in faith, we can become a child of God. As John 1:12," says"But as many as received Him, to them He gave the [a]right to become children of God, to those who believe in His name:"(see also Galatians 3:26). Notice in the verse, it says we have a "right" to become a child of God. It's your right to be a child of creation and through the cross to now choose to be a spiritual child of God. Why do we have to choose it? Because this is a special sonship that is not simply imposed on you, you have to want it. You have to choose to be part of this adoption process. Really, doesn't this make it even more beautiful? When an older child is adopted and freely chooses to be adopted, it makes the adoption so much more special for them and the adoptive parents.

It's by God's love that we can choose this special adoption as his children. As I John 3:1, says, "Behold what manner of love the Father has bestowed on us, that we should be called children of

[a]God! Therefore the world does not know [b]us, because it did not know Him." It's the highest honor to become a spiritual child of God. Something we should be excited to embrace. Something that we should be forever grateful for the opportunity to be his child.

The next verse says, "Beloved, now we are children of God; and it has not yet been revealed what we shall be, but we know that when He is revealed, we shall be like Him, for we shall see Him as He is." The full mystery of what it means to be a child of God is not even fully known or understood. We will be like Him, which is amazing in itself. We shall be fully glorified as Christ is. We can start the process now though of being like Him. Everything we need to be like Him is within us right now. It's a matter of processing and manifesting it!

Becoming a child of God and knowing who we are will give us great hope, both now and for eternity. Verse 3 says, "And everyone who has this hope in Him purifies Himself, just as He is pure." This hope of being like Christ and being made a child of God is something that purifies us. It purifies us through the power of love and peace that we get from God. This will keep you from darkness and sin. Daily focus on becoming like Him and embracing your sonship or daughtership. Yes, we decide one day to be a child of God, but we can embrace it and meditate on it every day and receive hope!

When you choose to be a child of God, everything in your life changes, as we saw in II Corinthians 5:17: "Therefore, if anyone is in Christ, he is a new creation; old things have passed away; behold, all things have become new." Allow yourself to become renewed every day by this truth! You're a new creation! Ephesians 4:24 tells us what the new man entails "and that you put on the new man which was created according to God, in true righteousness and holiness." The new creation's life is one of true righteousness. This righteousness encompasses the fruits of the Holy Spirit and much more!

Things we did in the past may haunt us. Things others did may haunt us in the past, but when you really start to meditate on the fact that you are a new creation, you can release those thoughts. You can know that those issues are washed away. You aren't the same person who you were then. Let those pains go. Even if you were a believer when you did those things, or when it happened to you, let them be washed away, as you are renewed each day. The new creation life starts at your conversion. It doesn't end there. In an actual sense, the new creation life is a continuous process that never stops. You are being made new, present tense. I was meditating on this just now in my meditation time. It's much like starting out as a large rock. The sculptor keeps chiseling away. With each cut and chisel, we see something new. More is revealed to us as he or she works. A nose, then a mouth, now a complete face. Then hands. It just keeps growing until we transcend into the next world.

As a spiritual child of God, you will inherit everything from Christ and with Christ, Romans 8:17 says, "and if children, then heirs—heirs of God and joint-heirs with Christ, if indeed we suffer with Him, that we may also be glorified together." We will have the right to all things and rule with Christ. (see II Timothy 2:12)

We often talk about being God's servant, but as a child of God, we are so much more than that. John 15:15 says, "No longer do I call you servants, for a servant does not know what his master is doing; but I have called you friends, for all things that I heard from My Father I have made known to you." I really love this verse. I am the friend of Christ. He isn't just a master that sits over me, but a friend that walks by the side of me.

WE HAVE ALL POWER IN CHRIST

Through His Spirit, we have all the power of God within us. Acts 1:8 says," But you shall receive power when the Holy Spirit has come upon you, and you shall be [a]witnesses to Me in

Jerusalem, and in all Judea and Samaria, and to the end of the earth." This power gives us the spiritual authority to act and to teach the nations of God. The Spirit is present within us to teach us all things that we need. John 14;26 says, "But the [g]Helper, the Holy Spirit, whom the Father will send in My name, He will teach you all things, and bring to your remembrance all things that I said to you." Remember, the Holy Spirit teaches through the word. How are we able to remember the things Christ taught us since we personally were not there? By the scriptures! Be in the scriptures for the Spirit to bring it back to your memory. Is it possible to have the Spirit teach us directly within our spirits? Yes, but the teaching of the word is the primary source of our wisdom, so it makes sense to also be familiar with it and not rely on just a direct Spirit teaching. Sometimes the Spirit will teach you something, and then you may discover it later as you go through the word. That does sometimes happen.

We have the power to walk in his Light through the Spirit as well. I remember the account of Dannion Brinkley's near-death experience, where He went to heaven after being struck by lightning. He was told that He was a powerful spiritual being. This goes along with scripture. By embracing the Spirit, we open up our source of power within our souls. I often use this as an affirmation as well as in my meditation. I say, "I am a powerful spiritual being!" Sometimes I look at others and affirm their power as well. Open the door to your power and begin to operate in this power!

Through Christ, we can do anything. Philippians 4:13 says, "I can do all things through [a]Christ who strengthens me." This has been one of my favorite verses for many years. This, too, is one I use as an affirmation. All things through Christ's power are possible. This is where the moving of spiritual mountains comes in.

Through Christ, we are complete in our spiritual being. There isn't anything we now need to walk in the Light, it's simply a matter of manifesting it. Col 2:10 says, "and you are complete in Him, who is the head of all [a]principality and power." We through Christ can take down any principality or power that comes against us. I believe in demons, but honestly, I really don't spend too much of my time focusing on them. There are some churches and Christians that spend a great deal of time talking about the devil and demons. I don't really know why. As you operate in his power and begin to produce the fruits of the Spirit, you take away the demonic powers that would ever come against you. The dark forces don't like to be around love, kindness, and peace. I truly believe they feed off fear and other negative qualities. Possibly in some literal way. If you want demons around you, give in to fear, hatred, etc. You can cast demons out, but often I found the easiest way to keep them from coming around in the first place is through fully embracing unconditional love. When I was younger, I spent time casting demons out and binding Satan. Now I just focus on love and they don't seem to come around so much.

Much of our victory over sin and Satan comes through the fact that we are already victors. We don't need to sweat it, just live in His Light. Romans 8:37 says, "Yet in all these things we are more than conquerors through Him who loved us." Recognize the fact that you are already the conqueror, you don't need to conquer anything. If you have a sin that you can't seem to beat, it's a matter of realizing who you are already and walking in that power. Don't believe the lies or the false identity you may get from Satan, this world, or your own mind. Allow your perception to change. Stop seeing yourself as this defeated sinner but a powerful, complete, victorious child of God that can do anything through Christ.

Because of God's power within us, we have a beautiful and bright future set before us. Jeremiah 29:11 says, "For I know the thoughts that I think toward you, says the Lord, thoughts of peace and not of evil, to give you a future and a hope." It's not a matter if we will win, but it is the fact that we have won already and will have a glorious eternity with Him. This eternity doesn't start when we die but starts now. Believe in this hope and watch the beautiful picture unfold before you!

WE ARE SEATED WITH CHRIST IN HEAVEN

We had discussed the Kingdom of God is within us earlier. Heaven is within our soul and is primarily the qualities of love, peace, and righteousness. Yes, we go to higher realms when we die within our spirit, but these realms are spiritual and always with us. This includes right now. The only difference is that we shred our physical body and take on a spiritual one. I like to say our body is the only thing that dies, not us. When we die, the distractions of the body and this world go, and we see and experience things in the spiritual realm more clearly. As I heard one person say, we live out of our souls completely when the body is gone.

Ephesians 2:6 says, "raised us up together, and made us sit together in the heavenly places in Christ Jesus." Notice the verse puts it within the present moment. Not that we will be seated, but that we are seated now in heaven. The journey in heaven doesn't start the day your heart stops beating but when you embrace His Light. It's like the key is turned and the heavenly dimension within us is now opened. This heaven within us will continue for eternity. The next verse speaks of the ages to come in Christ, but heaven within us starts immediately.

Since we are already in heaven within our being, our actual home is heaven. We became citizens of heaven. Philippians 3:20 says, "For our citizenship is in heaven, from which we also eagerly wait for the Savior, the Lord Jesus Christ,". Yes, we await the return of Jesus to earth in his second coming, that is future tense. The citizenship in heaven, however, like being seated in heaven, is present tense. When you really start to grasp that you are truly in heaven now, this can help to change your perspective on life. Heaven is the realm of love, this is the essence within your soul. I genuinely believe that the true essence of every person is love. This is the core of our being. Most don't realize this. Most have some level of darkness that covers it from view, but in no way does it change this reality. As a believer, we have opened the door and turned on the lights to this reality. Now walk in it!

WE REPRESENT GOD ON THE EARTH

We are not just citizens of heaven but ambassadors for heaven. We personally represent God on earth. In II Corinthians 5:20 it says, "Now then, we are ambassadors for Christ, as though God were pleading through us: we implore *you* on Christ's behalf, be reconciled to God." When an ambassador is sent by a nation, he or she represents the king or head of state of that nation. We operate personally in the power and authority of God. This both should excite us and make us pause as well. This is an awesome gift and responsibility. We should never take our duty as ambassadors lightly, but with reverence. We should always seek to do our best with His strength to positively represent Christ.

What are our duties as his representative? Well, to share love, kindness, and compassion, of course, but also to help to reconcile people back to God. We want to help people make peace with God through Christ. So we are also counselors and peacemakers as well. So we seek to live at peace with all people. (see Romans 12:18), but more importantly, to bring peace to them. Peace for their souls, but also peace with the giver of their souls! Jesus said in Matthew 5:9 "Blessed *are* the peacemakers, For they shall be called sons of God." We are blessed if we are peacemakers. This has to include helping people to find peace with God as his ambassadors.

We help people to find peace by sharing Christ and his way of love, but we want to go deeper. Remember, the great commission is to make disciples. Mathew 28:19 says, "Go [c]therefore and make disciples of all the nations, baptizing them in the name of the Father and of the Son and of the Holy Spirit," We have a commission as his ambassador to disciple the world in his teachings which center on love. We are also to immerse them in this love, which is pictured in the ordinance of baptism.

As God's representatives on earth, we don't do our work alone, but with all believers. God has made us a nation of people to represent Him on earth. I Peter 2:9 says, "But you *are* a chosen generation, a royal priesthood, a holy nation, His own special people, that you may proclaim the praises of Him who called you out of darkness into His marvelous light;" Just like the nation of Israel before us, and the priests of the Old Testament, we now operate as his chosen people on earth. This is a special calling that we have, and I believe the whole point of election in the New Testament. The election really isn't about us being the only ones who will be saved or the only people God loves, rather it's a special calling to go to the world in love. God wills all people to be saved and loves all people. I Timothy 2:4 says, "Who will have all men to be saved, and to come unto the knowledge of the truth." (KJV) The truth is for everyone, but He has his ministers to proclaim the message. We know God loves all because of John 3:16 "For God so loved the world that He gave His only begotten Son, that whoever believes in Him should not perish but have everlasting life." This love was present even before we believed, as we noted earlier. (see Romans 5:8)

CO-CREATORS WITH GOD

We co-create with God in a variety of ways. One way we co-create is by doing his work. I Corinthians 3:9, says," For we are God's fellow workers; you are God's field, *you are* God's building." We work alongside God to create and do new things in this world. I believe that part of what we will be doing in the ages to come is co-creating with God when He starts new worlds and continues to expand heaven. We will rule and reign with Him.

Part of being in the image of God is that, by our very nature, we are creative beings. We seek to create in virtually every way, including art and music. We also seek to create by innovation.

We were given dominion over the earth to care for it as stewards, but also to be creative in it. (Genesis 1:27, 28) We have created new species of plants and new breeds of animals, such as dogs. We have cross-bred many animals over the centuries. This all comes from a natural creative desire that was put within us as human beings. As long as our creative process doesn't harm but helps enrich the world, it can be a good thing.

As we saw before, we existed in some form for eternity in God. My personal belief is that our souls were created at the beginning of time. (see Jeremiah 1:5) I believe we may have participated in the creation with God. In Genesis 1:26, it says, "Then God said, "Let Us make man in Our image, according to Our likeness; let them have dominion over the fish of the sea, over the birds of the air, and over the cattle, over [a]all the earth and over every creeping thing that creeps on the earth." I believe the "us" may have been humans that were going to co-create our race with God in the beginning. Most would say this is the trinity. Some might say it's the angels. I believe in the trinity, but it seems odd for God to speak to Himself in a plural form, even taking the trinity into account. If we are a part of God and take on his image, we may have been the "us" in the verse. We have a distinct identity from each other and God as a whole. We have our own awareness. This, of course, is my own speculation, and nothing I am promoting it dogmatically. Might we help to create or form a new race of beings on another planet at some time in the future, though in the ages to come? This might be when our world reaches its consummation. I think about this often.

Application

1. Take each section of this chapter and create one affirmation for it. Examples could be "I am a child of God", "I am a powerful spiritual being", "I am an ambassador to the king". Say these affirmations as your affirmations for the next week. You can do these affirmations in the morning, might, and throughout the day if you like. You can also take them into your

meditation time. Remember to repeat them at least 10 times before moving on to the next one.

2. Go through each section and find a key verse quoted above for who you are and what you have. It might be like "I can do all things through [a]Christ who strengthens me" (Philippians 4:13). Commit at least 3 to memory. Take the verses you memorize into your meditation. You can recite them, but also ponder them. You can visualize them in your life. See yourself in those verses

9. NO DISTRACTIONS!

"Let your eyes look straight ahead; fix your gaze directly before you. Give careful thought to the[a] paths for your feet and be steadfast in all your ways. Do not turn to the right or the left; keep your foot from evil." (Proverbs 4:25-27)

We live in a world with millions of voices telling us to go here or go there. Do this or do that. Believe this way or that way. It can often be overwhelming and confusing. What should you do and who can you trust? Sometimes the voices are direct and in your face. Other times they're more subtle. We have messages being given to us virtually every minute of the day. Some may be good, and some maybe not so good. With all these voices, for most comes distractions in their lives. Distractions from following God and doing what is in the best interest of you and those you love. Many today feel like they can't even feel their own voice amongst all the other voices out there. They certainly can't hear God's voice. Is it possible to hear within ourselves and also hear God with so much noise? Yes! But it will not always be easy and it's a matter of taking time to really stop, listen, and focus on what really is important.

The biggest issue we will probably face as children seeking to walk in the Light is not actually sin itself, but distractions. Yes, sin is often the result of being distracted, but the key is to keep our focus straight and stay on course. This will help to dramatically reduce the times we do fall into sin. The verse above is vital to our walk as a child of God. We must keep our eyes focused on God and the things of God. This is where things like meditation can be so helpful. We are able to focus our awareness on things like love and compassion. This is the essence of mindfulness, being present in each moment. We should always seek to be present with God in every moment. In Matthew 6:34 it says, "Therefore do not worry about tomorrow, for tomorrow will worry about its own things. Sufficient for the day is its own trouble." We need to not worry about what will come, nor should we live in the past. We often dwell on past mistakes which can bring us down in our walk. Our focus should be right now and doing everything to walk for Christ in this moment. Within our day, it's often a matter of focusing on the things of God and constantly refocusing on them. Any time I start to feel confused or like I'm going off track, even for a moment or only slightly, I consciously refocus on my main goal, which is love.

Prayer can also help us keep our focus on God throughout our day. Therefore we should have the mindset of prayer, praying continuously as well as having regular prayer times each day. Pray for focus and pray with a focus. Ephesians 5:15, 16 says, "See then that you walk [a]circumspectly, not as fools but as wise, 16 redeeming the time, because the days are evil." Be careful in how you live each moment. Not that we will have no worries, but to keep your attention always pointing toward the things of God.

Another way to keep from distractions and stay focused is to spend time in the scriptures as we have seen before. We have the tools we need with things like prayer, meditation, and the scriptures to not get distracted. It's also important to notice if you are becoming distracted and refocus.

THE PATH

If you're familiar with John Bunyan's "Pilgrim's Progress", you understand the importance of staying on the path that God has placed you on. In the story, Christian is told to stay on the path. Don't go to the right or left, don't detour, don't stop. Christian, of course, runs into all kinds of distractions along the way that takes him off course. In our own lives, people, situations, and even our own mind can cause us to go astray. It's usually not deliberate. Often we just realize down the line that we have gotten off the beaten path. Sometimes we don't know how to get back, or rationalize that we will eventually go back, but not at this time. How do we stay on the path? How do we get back on the path if we have strayed and become distracted?

Deuteronomy 5:33 says, " You shall walk in all the ways which the Lord your God has commanded you, that you may live and *that it may be* well with you, and *that* you may prolong *your* days in the land which you shall possess." The path is simply to walk in the ways of the Lord. Sounds simple, but what does that entail? We walk in his ways through the word, prayer, and meditation. We receive guidance through them, and it keeps our focus on Him.

One way to be on the right path is by always acknowledging God in all things. Proverbs 3:6, says "In all your ways acknowledge Him, And He shall [a]direct your paths." Acknowledging Him is more than just speaking of God and recognizing that He exists. It also requires that we follow Him. God is love, so the most obvious way to acknowledge Him is through love. This is something that the world sees as well. Yes, we follow all the scriptures, but the central point is love. This is what sums it all up, as we have seen. This is the point I am constantly coming back to in my own life. Sometimes even daily. When I begin to feel confused or overwhelmed, I immediately redirect myself to love and the qualities of love, such as compassion and kindness. Everything we do must go through love, even other "righteous" things we do for God. Without it, we can still become distracted, even if we appear to be walking on the right path on the outside. To walk on God's path is to walk both externally and internally. As you walk this path, allow yourself to be refreshed with His peace and joy, because this, too, will help you keep going and not get sidetracked. Our goal is always to be serving the Lord without distraction. (I Corinthians

7:35).

ANGER

One of the biggest distractions that can completely sidetrack your walk in the Light is anger. I know of many cases where marriages have ended effectively over this issue. Uncontrolled anger can lead to emotional and even physical abuse in extreme cases. Anger is not a trivial matter. Even Christians can fall prey to uncontrolled anger. I have had to learn to control my own anger over the years. I suspect many of you have as well or are working on improving in this area. Anger can negatively affect every area of your life. Unsurprisingly, we read in Psalm 37:8, "Cease from anger, and forsake wrath; Do not fret—it only causes harm." The ultimate goal is to cease from anger altogether. In most cases, it serves no useful purpose for ourselves or others around us. There may be times when we need to speak forcefully and strongly to get our point across, but even then, always seek to do so in a controlled, measured way. Hold your frustration in a balanced way.

Anger doesn't help us in any way to walk as a child of the Light. It does quite the opposite. James 1:20 says, "for the wrath of man does not produce the righteousness of God." Anger most times not only doesn't produce righteousness but can produce much unrighteousness. Anger can also destroy your health in the process, leading to greater stress and anxiety. Anger, like so many other vices such as bitterness, can literally poison our bodies and souls.

We want to be slow and careful in all that we do. In Proverbs 14:29 it says, "He who is slow to wrath has great understanding, But he who is [a]impulsive exalts folly." We want to be able to step back and take things slowly when we feel ourselves becoming upset. This is where meditation becomes so important in reducing our overall anger levels. It reduces our anger and thus makes us slower to anger. It will take more to really get us upset. Notice that the verse mentions impulse. So much anger goes to impulse control. People that have violent tempers generally lack good impulse control.[23] Meditation gives you better impulse control over time. Science has shown a connection between impulse control and anger. Learning to control impulses is a key element in anger management therapies. Interesting how scripture thousands of years ago pointed out the connection.

When you catch yourself becoming angry, you may not have time to go to a 30-minute meditation session. What you can do is do a mini-meditation of 1 to 3 minutes, or at least take a few deep breaths. Breathe in through the nose deeply, hold for 8 seconds, and then exhale through the mouth. We discussed this earlier, but it can help in the moment. You can also start to pray and ask God for help, tell Him how you are feeling at that moment. Sometimes simply expressing to God how you feel can be cathartic in itself.

One aspect of reducing anger is cultivating the fruit of gentleness. Proverbs 15:1 says A soft answer turns away wrath, But a harsh word stirs up anger. A soft word is a gentle word. So much of our society revolves around speaking harshly with each other. You see this in movies and TV, we all applaud when someone tells another person off, often using harsh and inflammatory words to do so. When you speak harshly with others and really tell them off, you're feeding into anger and often causing more harm than good. Seek to speak more gently with others, and always seek to speak with compassion and empathy, even when you need to express your disapproval to someone. You may need to speak plainly, but you don't need to speak cruelly or crudely to them.

Something that might seem contradictory is a passage that says to be angry and sin not. We are told to put away anger and how terrible anger is in other passages. Ephesians 4:26, 27 says, "Be angry, and do not sin": do not let the sun go down on your wrath," How do we make sense of this? Just a few verses later, Paul says in Ephesians 4:31, "Let all bitterness, wrath, anger, [a]clamor, and evil speaking be put away from you, with all malice." The key might be that the word for anger in verse 26 is a different word than in verse 31. From looking at other verses, the word anger in verse 31 is often associated with wrath or a violent passion, sometimes vengeance. The Greek word is orgē. The Strongs number is 3709.[24] The word in verse 26 is orgizō which is Strong's number 3710. This word is connected to being provoked and may have more of a context of being upset.[25] Orgizō may be more justified because it is provoked and it's probably a lesser degree of anger. We will all get upset sometimes in our lives, but we don't want to let it go into a more vicious form of anger. Even with this more mild form of anger, we still want to let it go as quickly as possible, which is why the verse says don't let the sunset on your anger and seek to reconcile quickly. Again, prayer and meditation can help to let us release all anger, regardless of how intense it may be. You can release it to God.

FEAR

Fear is one of the biggest distractions that we can have in our walk, if not the biggest. I know from my own life, fear has often crippled me in doing what God would want me to do. If you're honest, it has most likely hindered your walk. Millions of people from virtually every nation on earth were gripped with fear over the last few years of a certain "pandemic". The biggest pandemic, of course, was a pandemic of fear. Some may not realize that the opposite of love is not hatred, but fear. Much of the problems we see in the world today are rooted in fear, including hatred itself. Many of the other distractions, such as pride mentioned in this chapter, have some connection back to fear. We fear we will not have what we need or fear losing our reputation with others. We fear the consequences of not acting in a certain way. Ultimately, we fear death itself. The scriptures teach a common reason for fear as well as the cure for it. I John 4:18 says, "There is no fear in love, but perfect love casts out fear because fear involves torment. But he who fears has not been made perfect in love." This is one of my favorite verses in all of scripture. It's a verse I do in my own affirmations and meditations. "Perfect love casts out all fear". This may not be something we want to hear or believe, but the reason we live in so much fear boils down to a lack of love or a love that has not been perfected. This is something to really pray and meditate on. You can make the shortened version of "perfect love casts out all fear" one of your affirmations as well.

One way to perfect our love and release the fear is by praying about anything that we fear or feel anxious about. Phil 4:6,7 says, "Be anxious for nothing, but in everything by prayer and supplication, with thanksgiving, let your requests be made known to God;" In continual prayer, we have a way to consciously release stress and anxiety to God. We can also do this within meditation as well. Next time you're in meditation, visualize yourself releasing your anxiety to God.

One key to being mindful in meditation is to be present, not focused on the past or future, but on right now. Not that we give no thought to the past or where we are going in the future, but it's not the principal place we want to be in our minds. Matthew 6:34 says, "Therefore do not worry about tomorrow, for tomorrow will worry about its own things. Sufficient for the day *is* its own trouble." It's important to be present because failures of the past or worries of the future can disempower us. You have enough on your plate at this moment. A key to being happy is to be as present as possible. If you can be within this day, good. If you can be within this hour, great. If you can be within this given moment, excellent!

LUST

There are three ways that lust can distract us from our mission. I John 2:16 says, "For all that *is* in the world—the lust of the flesh, the lust of the eyes, and the pride of life—is not of the Father but is of the world." The lust of the eyes can obviously be sexual lust, but it can also be lust after material things. In today's world, materialism is everywhere. We seek to have possessions. We want the best cars, homes, phones, games, etc. There isn't anything wrong with those things, but it can become a problem with our possessions, or the desire for them actually possesses us. This is where meditation comes into play. We can start to detach from desires that become overwhelming if we aren't focused. The power of observation is to step outside ourselves and objectively evaluate the thing that we are desiring so badly. Often, simply doing a detached observation can help to reduce the desire to a more manageable state. We do need to be honest with our desires, never try to suppress or repress them, but simply objectively observe them. Is this even what you actually want, or is it something you want because you believe it will give you a certain feeling? If the desire to have it is because it will make you happy, can you find happiness within yourself right now whether or not you have such a possession?

The lust of the flesh goes to many things as well, which can include sex, food, substances like alcohol or drugs, etc. The same things said above often apply here. In most cases, such things are not sinful in themselves, though sometimes they can be. Take time in meditation to observe the desires objectively and ask questions here as well. Ask, also what is really in my best interest and those that I love and care for. This will help you to keep things in perspective.

Pride is a huge issue in our society and has been a problem within humanity for thousands of years. It goes to the issue of vanity. We want to feel important or that we are better in some way than others. There can even be a one-upmanship with spiritual things if we aren't careful. We may secretly think that we are more holy, spiritual, or even loving than someone else, or even most people. This too can create a pride just as wealth and possessions can. We need to continually be reminding ourselves that life is not a competition. We in actuality, are no better or worse than anyone else. Our desire should be to be the best version of ourselves. We only compete against ourselves. We only compare ourselves to where we have been. Hopefully, we do see progress, but even there, it should be a point to thank God rather than brag about ourselves.

ROUTINE

Having a routine can in life be a double-edged sword in terms of distraction. On the one hand, it can get you going on some great things to help keep you from getting distracted. You can have a set time for prayer, meditation, reading scripture, etc. These are excellent tools to keep you focused on what is important. If you're not careful, though, it can become things you do with little thought. You start just going through the motions. You're there doing the right things, but your heart and mind may not be fully in it. Jesus said in Matthew 6:7, "And when you pray, do not use vain repetitions as the heathen do. For they think that they will be heard for their many words." Obviously, we don't need to be redundant with God but notice the word vain. It's not just repeating things that are the problem but doing so vainly. We can do positive affirmations. I don't think anything is wrong with them. We can pray for things over and over. The point is that they don't become just a ritual that we mindlessly do. You have to always put your heart and soul into it. Even if it's the 600th time you've prayed about this.

How do you put your heart back into it? One thing is to incorporate variety from time to time. Change up the routine even if just slightly. If you need to change the music you meditate to, or change the order you pray for things, do it. If you need to take a break from the section you are reading in scripture and read something else in scripture, do it. Basically, keep things fresh.

Second, take a moment to stop and really think about what you're doing. If you're praying about the same thing, ruminate about it. Allow yourself to feel some emotion in it as you pray. Sometimes elaborate on what you're doing. If you're praying for someone's healing, go into some detail with God as you pray. This may help you to feel the issue within you more deeply again. If you're reading scripture, seek to ask yourself how I can in some way apply this to my life. You can always ask God to help you not fall into ritual as well.

THE MULTITUDE OF VOICES

Today, it seems like there are a multitude of voices trying to pull you in a million directions. It's been this way for quite some time, but with advances in technology, it's intensified. Buy this product, go see this movie, follow this person, believe this way, act this way. The clamor for our attention can be overwhelming at times. We don't just have radio, TV, and magazines, but now we have the internet that is constantly available with the cell phone in our pockets. We are literally always wired into the world. We can know what anyone is thinking at virtually any moment. The media, government, and corporations study exactly how they can literally hypnotize us to act in a certain way. They play on our fears, lusts, pride, and simply wanting to fit in. Part of what we need to do is have times where we turn it all off. Turn off the phone, computers, TV, etc and be present with ourselves and others. Another aspect is to tune into the things of God with prayer, meditation, and the scriptures. Take time to hear from God and evaluate what you're being exposed to. Question everything.

Romans 12:2 says, "And do not be conformed to this world, but be transformed by the renewing of your mind, that you may prove what *is* that good and acceptable and perfect will of God." The goal of the believer is not to be conformed to the world but to the things of God. Some things in the world may be outright sins, but much of it in itself is not. However, constantly following the multitude of voices can still distract us from the more important things that God wants for us.

With all the voices come thoughts, it reminds me of this verse in II Corinthians 10:5 "casting down arguments and every high thing that exalts itself against the knowledge of God, bringing every thought into captivity to the obedience of Christ," A key to not being distracted is to bring all your thoughts to the captivity of Christ. You can do this while in meditation.

Application

1. What are the biggest distractions to walking as a child of the Light for you? Is it anger, fear, lust, routine, too many voices, or something not even mentioned in this chapter? Write this down as well as some things you can do to not get distracted by it, but bring it captive to God.

2. Are there things in your past that distracted you from your walk but now tend not to distract you anymore? If so, what did you do to help reduce their distraction?

10. AFFIRM YOUR GRATITUDE

"Oh, give thanks to the Lord, for He is good! For His [a]mercy endures forever." (Psalms 107:1)

Gratitude is one of the most important things if we are to walk as a child of the Light. If you want to transform your heart and mind, start to practice gratitude. It will empower you to live out your faith and walk in love. It will help to develop greater kindness within you. Gratitude is something that should be an integral part of both our prayer lives and our meditation time.

Who should we be expressing gratitude to? We should express it to God first and foremost. Most of this chapter revolves around showing gratefulness to God in all things. Ultimately, all things in our life, including our blessings, flow from God. We should also show gratitude toward those around us. Yes, if they are blessing us or giving us something that we need or want, but you can also express gratitude for what they may be teaching you even if by negative example. You can be grateful for their presence in your life and what good will come from having them in your life, both for you and them. You should show gratitude to yourself. As you are grateful for who you are and what you do, it will flow into gratitude toward God and others. Remember the circle of love? The same applies to gratitude. Be grateful in all circumstances as well. Everything in your life has value in one form or another.

BE GRATEFUL IN ALL THINGS

We are to be grateful in all things. I Thessalonians 5:18 says, "in everything give thanks; for this is the will of God in Christ Jesus for you" You notice that we are to be thankful in everything, absolutely nothing is left out in this verse. It's not just some things in our lives, or even most things but all things in our life. This includes being thankful for all circumstances and situations in our life. All people even includes being thankful for ourselves. Does this even mean being grateful for a cancer diagnosis? Does this mean being thankful for the person who hates us and makes our life miserable? Many will think "yes, I totally get being thankful for all my gifts and blessings but those kinds of things too?" The answer is yes! I read a book almost 30 years ago called "Prison to Praise" written by Merlin R. Carothers which advocated this very idea. Many that I shared the book with liked the book but would say this was just too extreme. I can be grateful through all things, but to be grateful for all things was just too much. Carothers went through the book showing how people were blessed as they just started to do this. I think he was on to something. If we want to really take our walk to the next level, we have to see beyond temporal circumstances and see that everything serves a larger purpose. If you can see that your worst times can be something to be grateful for, then gratitude in everything else is a cakewalk.

Remember Paul, who wrote the above verse, was actually grateful for the beatings and suffering he endured in the book of Acts (Acts 16) A cancer diagnosis is a time to draw closer to God and refine our Light. It's also a time to celebrate the real possibility of going home to heaven quicker than we thought. Even when a loved one has it, it's their time possibly to go home quicker. When you can see eternity and your perfection in it, the trials have less power over you.

Who are we to be grateful to? Well, God, of course, most of this chapter is about this. God is the ultimate source of all things. I think it also includes being grateful to others. Whether others are blessing or cursing us, they are giving us a chance to grow in the Light. For this, we can be grateful to them. Being grateful for what others do for us is also a way to show gratitude to God because it is God who has brought them into our lives. Just as Jesus said, "what you do unto the least of these, you do unto me" can apply to our service, so to can it apply to our gratitude toward them. Gratitude shown by others can bless and transform people. How do you feel when someone shows you gratitude for something you have done? In many cases, it can feel wonderful. Gratitude is another way we show love toward others, just like kindness and compassion. It is, in fact, a form of kindness itself.

You should also show gratitude to yourself and what you do. You are a representation of God too, so showing gratitude toward yourself is showing gratitude toward God. Be grateful for what you do to shine forth light and do anything that is good. Be grateful for who you are and what God has done in you. Be grateful for even small blessings that your mind and body do for you each day? Have you ever thanked your heart for beating and pumping blood to the rest of your body? Have you ever thanked your body for the power of breath, which brings oxygen to the rest of your body and makes life possible? If you can see, hear, smell, taste, or touch, thank God, but also thank the body you have that is currently allowing you to be able to do these things.

As you learn gratitude in all things, it can radically change your world. It's right up there with love itself in importance to walk as a child of the Light. Get radical with your gratitude, even if it seems crazy or silly, it's better to go overboard (not really even possible) than to be too cautious or conservative with it. Try praising and thanking God, others, and yourself for literally everything. Meditation and prayer are two great times to let loose in expressing your gratitude. Don't just say "I'm grateful for" or "thank you for", but really stop to embrace the feeling. Take the gratitude deep within your soul!

START EACH DAY WITH GRATITUDE TOWARD GOD

We should express gratitude every day. Psalms 118:24, says, "This *is* the day the Lord has made; We will rejoice and be glad in it." Gratitude is something we should do on a regular basis, day by day, moment by moment. I do daily affirmations each day. I do them upon first waking up and when I go to bed at night, along with my prayers. Part of my affirmations is affirming who I am and what I want. Another part, though, is expressing what I am grateful for. These affirmations of gratitude can be expressed as what I'm grateful for, as well as what I find beauty, dignity, and acceptance in all things. When I say "the acceptance of all things", I'm expressing gratitude for how things are in this exact moment. I can also express the beauty in all things, which is to say I am grateful for how lovely things are in this moment. Notice the verse above says to be glad in it. Anything that makes you feel happy or brings you joy can be seen as an expression of gratitude. So it's broader than just saying I'm grateful for this or that". Try to find happiness in all things as you go about your day and in everything in your life. Yes, look for the silver lining if that helps you. Affirmations during rising and setting are good because your mind and heart are more open to absorbing your words. It's also the first and last thing you dwell on in a day. So always start and end your day on a positive note, and gratitude is one of the best ways to do this.

Another time to express gratitude is in prayer. This one may be the most obvious. When you're talking to God, simply thank Him for all the things in your life. Sometimes I will take entire prayer sessions or days to exclusively only express my thankfulness to God and ask for nothing. You can also thank God as you go about your day. Whether or not it's an answered prayer, you can be assured God has probably lined it up for you.

Meditation is another great time for focusing on gratitude.

Both in terms of affirmations about what you're grateful for, but also focusing on things that bring you happiness, such as love and beauty. In meditation and prayer, really allow yourself to feel the gratitude deep within your being. This is probably easiest within meditation but can be done in prayer as well.

Closely connected to meditation, is simply being mindful as you go about your day of things you're grateful for or could be. Stop to reflect and focus on things in your life. It can be as simple as a warm day, pretty flowers, or a cold drink. Savor the goodness in each moment.

Within your interactions with others during the day, be mindful there as well, to express gratitude to other people. You may say "thank you" or "I appreciate that". You may also express joy and happiness for what someone else has done for you. This can be just as meaningful as letting someone know you appreciate them. When your child expresses excitement for something you do or give to them, that goes just as far as a direct thank you in most cases.

WE RELEASE PEACE IN OUR HEARTS BY THANKFULNESS

There is a strong connection between having gratitude and inner peace within you. Colossians 3:15 says, "And let the peace of God rule in your hearts, to which also you were called in one body; and be thankful." As you become more grateful for things in your life, it naturally leads to greater peace in your life. Ungrateful people tend to have more stress and depression, which probably doesn't surprise anyone. As you begin to embrace gratitude about God, yourself, others, and the circumstances in your life a peace starts to come over you. With gratitude comes an acceptance of the things in your life. Gratitude allows you to release the negativity of complaining.

Gratitude also sets you free from envy and jealousy. Remember, the 9th commandment prohibits coveting your neighbor's things, which encompasses jealousy and envy. If you aren't jealous of others, including the circumstances in their life, you are walking in acceptance and can easily take on a more thankful heart. A spiritually mature person is one who can not only be grateful for what he or she has but what others have as well. Can you be grateful when others are happy and blessed, even when you aren't blessed in the same way? Once you can do this, you will reach new levels of peace within your soul.

GIVE THANKS TO GOD FOR HIS GOODNESS

One of the main reasons we are to be grateful is because of God's goodness. Psalms 107:1 says, "Oh, give thanks to the LORD, for He is good! For His mercy endures forever." We constantly hear that God is good. We know that's what is expected of us as Christians to believe. Do you actually believe that God is good, though? Really, be honest with yourself and God for a moment. Part of seeing God as good has to start with honesty. If you don't see Him as good, talk to Him in prayer. Try to write down what you think isn't good about God and ask Him about it. Tell Him how you honestly feel and ask Him to show you the truth. We all probably believe at some level God is good, but often we don't always feel it. Are you upset with God about something? Did He take someone you love from you in a death? Is your health poor right now? When you express honest emotions to God, often it can be cathartic and can help you release bitterness and anger within your being. Being religious and pretending it isn't there is not going to help you become more grateful. Being real can help, however.

If you are convinced that God is good, without reservations, then you can begin to list why He is good. Write it down and take it into prayer and meditation so that you can expand your gratitude. This list can also help you if you're not 100% convinced as well, though. Honesty and listing out His goodness are essential to growing in your gratefulness to God. You may even find it helps with yourself and others as well.

Notice the thing listed why we should be grateful to God is because He is merciful. This mercy goes on forever. Do you truly believe and understand this idea? This, too, maybe something to go to God in prayer and meditation. Ask Him to give you a better understanding of what his eternal mercy means. You may have to go beyond what you've been taught about God or your current understanding, but once you do, so too will your gratitude toward God.

THANK GOD FOR HE GIVES US POWER AND BLESSING

God has generously given all things to us as believers. Nothing truly is lacking. As it says in II Corinthians 9:11" while *you are* enriched in everything for all liberality, which causes thanksgiving through us to God." Remember we had discussed the fact that we were empowered with everything we need to live a successful Christian life in earlier chapters. All things pertaining to faith and godliness we have within us. It's a matter of manifesting them within our life. As we meditate on these qualities, they can be released in our life, much like opening up a vault containing gold, silver, and precious stones. Enough to make a person rich beyond comparison spiritually. We know these qualities include the fruits of the Spirit, such as love, joy, and peace among others. Once you truly begin to understand this, gratitude will naturally flow. Ask God to illuminate your heart on these matters. As you express gratitude, it also helps to release joy and happiness into your life as well as everything else. So gratitude flows from the riches God has already given us, but it also helps us to release them into our life, as we pointed out with peace. Thank God for love, joy, and peace, and see what he does in your heart!

We not only walk in blessings from God but in power itself. As II Corinthians 2:14, says, "Now thanks *be* to God who always leads us in triumph in Christ, and through us [a]diffuses the fragrance of His knowledge in every place." We can have victory in all things, whether it be trials, tribulations, sickness, or sin. God has given us the victory! This doesn't mean things will be a cakewalk or a garden of roses all the time, even when we do focus on our power within Him, but we will succeed. One way or another, we can be assured, it's a done deal, so praise Him for the victory. The power to walk as a Child of the Light is there. It's just a matter of realizing it and embracing it. If your heart can be illuminated by this fact, everything in this book can become your reality. We may not have superhuman powers like superman or spiderman, but we do have supernatural strength to fully walk in love and bring things under the power of love, which is way better than x-ray vision or flying!

GRATITUDE IS AN ACT OF WORSHIP

Expressing gratitude to God is an act of worship. Psalms 95:2 says, "Let us come before His presence with thanksgiving; Let us shout joyfully to Him with psalms." Have you ever thought of giving thanks and praise to God as an act of worship before? It's every bit an act of worship as praying or reading the Bible itself. Much of the Bible and Psalms, in particular, are about praising and thanking God. I can remember going to Calvary Chapel and singing Praise music in the 1980s. Much of the music was called "Maranatha Praise" . I found out later that most of the praise songs were taken directly from the book of Psalms. Many churches sing hymns extracted directly from the Psalms as well. Psalms give a pattern and attitude we should follow as it relates to praising God. Whether it be in song, prayer, meditation, or simply how we speak about God to others. It should be something we dwell on throughout the day.

I believe that not only is direct praise and thanksgiving to God an act of worship, but really, any expression of gratitude can be an act of worship as well. Set your focus on making it an act of worship to God. You feel grateful to another person, think also of God, because God brought that person into your life and equipped them to bless you. God may have also inspired them to bless you. Make gratitude a centerpiece in your worship of God

Worship actually means to show the feeling or expression of reverence and adoration toward God.[26] Gratitude is the highest expression of adoration. It also shows a high degree of reverence. Do you feel adored and revered when people show you gratitude? To some extent, you probably do. So does God! I adore and show respect to Him by thanking Him for all that He has done, will do, or is going to do in my life!

GRATITUDE WILL KEEP YOU FROM LOSING HEART

All things are done for our good to show forth his grace to us. Grace is unmerited favor. So ultimately, all things happen to show favor to us. This may not be evident in the moment, but we can rest on the fact that it is true. As we realize all things are done for our good, we can give thanks and not lose heart. As it says in II Corinthians 4:15, 16, "**15** For all things *are* for your sakes, that grace, having spread through the many, may cause thanksgiving to abound to the glory of God.**16** Therefore we do not lose heart. Even though our outward man is perishing, yet the inward *man* is being renewed day by day. What is losing heart? Despair, depression, and hopelessness. As we will see later, gratitude helps to combat depression. It can help to relieve depression but can also help it from ever setting into our hearts. Depression can lead to despair and a lack of hope. Within the practice of gratitude, we can find hope for a bright future. When you see someone who is suicidal, what is something you instantly notice? They see nothing good in their future. You can have a teenager who is suicidal about circumstances in his or her life. To us, we may think that in a few years, most of the issues he or she is concerned with will not even be present. Simply hold on, it will get better. Gratitude gives us the ability to see good in all things and it gives us the ability to hold on even when a storm hits. Even mini-storms where a spouse is upset with you hold on because it will usually pass. I've found this out over my almost

12 years of marriage. Resist the temptation to just get caught in the moment and step outside the situation. Realize how good your spouse is, and feel the love for them in that moment. Be grateful for them and what they mean to you in your life.

Notice the verse says the inward man is being renewed day by day. Again, this goes back to the importance of walking in the Light daily. Pray, meditate, love, and express gratitude each and every day. It will become ingrained in your being as you do these things. Gratitude renews us each day.

THANKFULNESS WILL GROUND YOU IN THE THINGS OF GOD

Gratitude is something that helps to ground us in our faith and helps to establish deep roots in our spiritual life. Colossians 2:7 says, "rooted and built up in Him and established in the faith, as you have been taught, abounding [a]in it with thanksgiving." Notice the connection between faith and gratitude in this verse. As it established us in our faith, gratitude naturally abounds. Gratitude also helps to strengthen our faith so that we are mature in the faith. Jesus spoke of allowing our seeds to fall in the good soil and go deep. We looked at this in the first chapter of this book. Gratitude helps to give us good soil for our seeds of faith, as well as helping those seeds to be planted deep within our hearts. Gratitude is much like love in that it's an essential ingredient to producing a living faith. Really, gratitude, like kindness, is an aspect of love itself. You show love when we are grateful. If you really want to go deep with God, practice gratitude with God and in all areas of your life.

SCIENTIFIC BENEFITS OF GRATITUDE

Besides being something commanded in scripture as well as commended, there're actually many benefits of gratitude that are now being recognized by psychologists and other health professionals. These benefits are being demonstrated in scientific studies. One benefit of gratitude is that it can help to bring more positive relationships into your life. If you want to make more friends or find that special person, gratitude is a great way to help make this happen. It can also help to improve the current relationships you already have with family and friends. This makes logical sense. What kind of person do you like to be around? A person who is optimistic and grateful, or one that is constantly complaining? Most of us are obviously attracted to grateful people. We have spoken of being grateful to God throughout this chapter, but be grateful for what others are doing for you or with you. Let them know you are grateful and appreciate them. Showing gratitude toward others can often change the direction of their day and the tone of your interaction with them. A study actually found that when people first meet you, they are more likely to want to form a relationship with you if you express gratefulness to them, such as thanking them. I've gotten into the habit of always thanking the employees at stores such as the cashiers. I worked as a cashier and got in the habit of thanking the customers and wishing them a good day. Now I do it with the cashier as a customer. I can tell that they appreciate it, sometimes are even a bit surprised.

Being grateful can make you physically healthier. Stress and negativity not only take a toll on your mental health but can start to affect your physical health as well. When you're grateful, you're happier which can release positive chemicals into your body. A 2012 study found that people who are grateful experience fewer aches and pains. This may be because of a release of endorphins. A grateful person tends to take better care of their physical health. This is important because our bodies are the temple of God. (I Corinthians 6:19, 20) Being grateful indirectly helps us to be better stewards of what the body has given us.

Gratitude helps to reduce negative toxic emotions, such as envy, resentment, regret, and frustration. It has been shown to even help with stress, anxiety, and depression, even to the point of helping people who suffer from post-traumatic stress disorder (PTSD). Gratitude makes us happier and helps to give us a greater sense of well-being.

Grateful people are more likely to have more empathy and less aggression. Studies have shown that even when presented with negative treatment by others, grateful people are less likely to seek revenge or retaliate. If you are trying to live as Christ taught, to return good for evil, and turn the other cheek to those that would abuse you, you should seek to cultivate a grateful heart. Gratitude is essential for those that want to be like Christ and work as a child of the Light. Gratitude will help to give you greater emotional control. This is critical when dealing with your spouse or children. To be less reactionary is a blessing. It's something I've worked on for years, and it has helped by aiding me to develop a more grateful perspective. If you can also recognize the blessings when challenges come and know that it's going to be ok, you will go a long way in helping to become a more peaceful, gentle person.

Being a grateful person can help you sleep better. A study found that keeping a gratitude journal and writing down a few things you're grateful for can help you to sleep longer and more soundly. I have recommended keeping a journal in this book and in my meditation book and courses. When you sleep better, you feel better. You're more motivated to serve God and others.

If you want to improve your self-esteem, gratitude will help you do this. A study found that athletes who are grateful had higher levels of self—esteem and improved their performance. This could help you improve your performance at work or school as well. Grateful people compare themselves less to other people and can more easily appreciate the accomplishments of others. Gratitude thus reduces envy and jealousy, which is vital if you want to walk as a child of the Light.

Gratefulness helps you to be a mentally stronger person. You are also more resilient when bouncing back from difficult circumstances that will arise in your life.[27] We may not be able to totally avoid all negative feelings all the time. We may still become angry or down, but we can know that gratitude will not only help to reduce these feelings but will help us recover faster from them. To walk as a child of the Light, we have to be able to bounce back quickly when we fall and get back in the game we're in. Paul compares the Christian life to a race. If you're a runner that falls, you need to get back up and keep going if you fall. (I Corinthians 9:24, 25). Gratitude is one tool in your toolbox to quickly get back in that race and win!

Application

1. Pull out your journal and make a list of all the things you're grateful for. You can break it down into areas of your life. Finances, health, relationships, emotions, and your spiritual life. Even if you're having some serious challenges in some of those areas, you can easily find some good points to write down. Try to come up with at least 5 things you're grateful for from each section.

2. Take your list into prayer and start to thank God for each and everything listed. You may even want to spend your entire prayer time for the next few days just praying about what you're grateful for.

3. Create at least 10 affirmations related to gratitude. They can include some of the things from your list but can also include things like love, compassion, kindness, beauty, etc. Take time within your meditation to focus on these affirmations. You may also focus on your list above and just allow yourself to really feel the gratitude within your heart and soul. Yes, it's good to attach positive emotions to them. It helps to enforce a more grateful mindset.

4. Consciously try to express more gratitude toward others for the next few days. Whether it's with your family and friends or just the cashier at the store. Genuinely express that

you appreciate them. Be sure to also convey it with your body language. Smile, show affection, or shake the person's hand if appropriate.

11. FIND INSPIRATION

"As a man thinketh, so is he." (Paraphrase of Proverbs 23:7 KJV)

So much of this book is about our focus in life. We've talked about the importance of prayer, meditation, and being in the word. These are the main things we want to be concentrating on in our walk with God. They're without question the most important things to be dwelling on in our hearts and minds. The reality is that the vast majority of your day is probably not going to be spent praying, meditating, and studying the scripture. Even if you gave an hour to each of these activities, which is way more than most of us will most likely give, that would be 3 hours of your day. What about the other 21 hours in a day, 8 of which you're sleeping? Yes, we should seek to create a more meditative life. We should seek to pray continuously. We should also seek to be pondering the scriptures as we go about our day. But we will fill most of our day with other thoughts if we're honest with ourselves.

Most of us don't have the luxury of living a monastic life where our primary activities each day are prayer, meditation, and scripture. You have work, family, and other obligations. We should seek to draw positive inspiration in the other areas of our life as well. What we watch on TV. What type of movies do we view? When consuming books and other reading materials outside of scripture, what do we read? What we listen to. Silence is golden, and it's a good idea to seek silence when you can, but for most of us, our day is consumed with noise coming from somewhere, even the "noise" when we're reading from the text.

You've probably heard many sermons over your lifetime that tell you what you should not watch, or what you shouldn't read or listen to. This isn't my focus here at all. This is not a legalistic rant about what not to take in, but possibly what you may want to take in. Rather than obsessing over the negative, the point is to accentuate the positive in all areas of what we consume. As you walk more in the Light, the negative things will become less and less attractive to you. The violent, vulgar, and profane will not appeal to you as it once did. So what can I take in to uplift me in my walk? The point of consuming positive things outside the scriptures, prayer, and meditation is not to suggest that they ever replace them. Those three are essential and not replaceable. What these other forms of inspiration can do, though, is to buttress and support your time spent in prayer, meditation, and scripture.

PLANTING IN THE POSITIVE

We discussed Philippians 4:8 with meditation in chapter 3. In fact; it was our opening verse. The verse says "Finally, brethren, whatever things are true, whatever things are noble, whatever things are just, whatever things are pure, whatever things are lovely, whatever things are of good report, if there is any virtue and if there is anything praiseworthy—meditate on these things." The verse obviously applies to meditation, which is where we put our concentrated focus on something but can also apply to anything we dwell on, including the things we aren't paying much attention to. We are taking information all the time. This information makes its way into our subconscious and affects how we feel, think, and act. You often may not even be aware of it. So it's important to try to always be putting good things in because we are constantly planting seeds within our hearts, mind, and soul. The scriptures and meditation plant good seeds. Other inspirational programming can as well. Not everything you can put in is planting good seeds, however. This probably doesn't surprise you. As you think you become, which was our verse introducing this chapter.

If you look at Philippians 4:8, there are six things mentioned to dwell upon. The things are broad and give a person literally millions of things that can be focused on, but all things are positive. There should be no trouble finding things that interest you and that are not boring to take in.

The first thing you can focus on is truth. The Greek word is alēthēs which simply means to love the truth or be truthful. What does truth actually mean, though? Truth is dealing with reality. You can have fictional stories that deal with what is true or contain a truth in it. Jesus taught truths in his parables. Truth is also connected to light, where you shine a light on things so that they become plain or transparent. Transparency is something often lacking in our society. Yes, sometimes you have to think deeply to gain the truth, but it always becomes apparent at some point. The opposite of truth is deception, which is often mixed with confusion. We know who the author of confusion is. What we watch should seek to convey truth and light, never being deceptive.

The second quality is noble. The Greek word is semnos which means honorable, venerable, or to esteem highly. When you venerate something, you place a high value on it. Values to honor or venerate are ones such as the fruits of the Holy Spirit. Can you find programs or things to read that extol love, joy, peace, patience, kindness, goodness, faithfulness, gentleness, or self-control? If you can, you may very well have something worth taking in. When I think of a noble, I think of things that promote dignity or value in others. Seeing dignity in all people is a noble virtue. Things that degrade overs, not so much. One way you promote the dignity of others is through compassion. Anything that promotes compassion honors the dignity of that person and is noble.

The word for just in Greek is dikaios which means just, right or righteous. It's being virtuous or following the laws of God. When you think of the laws of God, what comes to mind? Probably the 10 commandments. This is a good starting point, but not all the laws of God are contained in the 10 commandments. Think about what you take in. Does it honor your parents? This could be both in how it portrays and how parents and elders are treated, but also would you be embarrassed to watch such a show or read a book with your parents in the room? Does the show honor life and faithfulness? Does it honor being truthful? Does it portray God in a positive or negative light if it brought God up in the program? How does it portray those seeking to follow God? Does it mock them or belittle them?

The word for pure in Greek is hagnos which is referring to being chased, clean, and free of carnality. The word pure in this verse clearly relates to sexuality. Sex is a common theme in entertainment today, and much of it is anything but pure. I don't believe that such entertainment has to be completely void of sexuality or a discussion of it to be clean. However, it should represent it in a way that conveys a wholesomeness to it if it brought the topic up. In most cases, you know instantly within your spirit if it's being shown in a way that is good or is only there to be sensual or provocative.

What does lovely refer to in this verse? The Greek word is prosphilēs which means to be pleasing and acceptable. The first thing that comes to mind when I hear lovely is something that's beautiful. This can refer to something that is beautiful to look at, such as scenes of nature. It can also refer to concepts and ideas that are beautiful as well. The ideas of love, compassion, and kindness are beautiful principles to see in a movie or show. They are beautiful to read about in a story. I also think of things that are peaceful. Things that can help to bring peace of mind, serenity, tranquility, or calmness are lovely to me. Anything pleasant is going to be lovely, provided it's in line with the things of God. Such things bring true happiness and joy into a person's life.

What does of "good report' refer to? The word in Greek is euphēmos which means giving a good word or speaking auspiciously. The Strongs uses the word auspiciously to define euphemos and it can speak of favorable circumstances or outcomes. It's an interesting word because most shows present the challenge followed by a triumph that is positive at the end.[28] They built adventure books and films on this concept. So they seek to capture an auspicious outcome. In some darker films today, the outcomes are not always as positive as they used to be, and even if it resolves out ok, it still may leave you feeling down. I really don't like the darker direction that some films have taken over the past few years. You see this with superhero movies quite often. They aren't as upbeat as they once were. Your soul is not uplifted. Not that every film has to close with a fairytale ending by any means. How can you tell accurate history in this way? There are many films like "Schindler's List "that just are not cheery. The stories need to be told, however. The word euphemos is where we get the word euphemism, which today doesn't have a good connotation. You're trying to soft-peddle something. This can happen, but the true context is to speak of unpleasant things discreetly, don't glorify the horror. The thing is, they rarely need to be told in a highly gory fashion that emphasizes violence, which is so true today in many films. They could also do a better job of emphasizing the heroes. When the heroes are presented, other values such as love, kindness, and compassion can be brought out, as well as courage.

YOUR FOCUS IS YOUR PERCEPTION

We discussed earlier that what you focus on can affect how you feel. It creates your perception of the world around you. Perception is everything in this life. Well, that might be a bit of an overstatement, but there's a great deal of truth in it. Happiness, joy, and peace are within you and are shaped by your perceptions. Circumstances themselves play only a minor role in our joy, happiness, and peace. It has more to do with our perception and focus within those circumstances. You can take two people going through the same circumstances and one is happy and at peace while the other is miserable.

What we take in has the power to affect our mood. We instinctively know this. Have you ever watched a movie or listened to a song that made you feel sad, depressed, sensual, or angry? The darkness in some programs or songs has such power. It shifts our focus in a negative direction. The same is true that it can also take us in a more positive direction. Have you ever watched something or heard a song that made you feel happy or at peace? It's difficult to not allow such programs or music to take us in a certain direction, which is why it's so important to choose wisely what we take in.

Look at the news. The news has the power to make you more fearful and distrusting of others. This is true whether we are talking about the mainstream media or alternative media. If you haven't noticed by now, humans gravitate toward fear, which can even go to the point of creating hysteria. I believe that is what we've witnessed with a certain virus lately. Limiting the news that you take in is probably a wise choice.

The same is true for social media. Much of what's on social media is negative and fear-based. I am speaking to myself because I spend a lot of time on it. It can promote worthwhile things, and you can find some positivity there, but you have to be careful. Sometimes it's helpful to take a day or week to just detox from social media and stay off. I've done this from time to time.

MUSIC TO UPLIFT YOUR SOUL

Music is one of the most dynamic ways to positively alter our emotions. Music can make you feel happier, calmer, and more at peace. It also has the power to take us down into more negative emotions, such as anger, lust, and sadness. So it's important that we seek to listen to music that will uplift our souls. You don't become more spiritual by listening to music, but it can affect how your spirit feels. It may affect how your spirit responds to the Spirit of God in you as well. As we have said, when we feel good, we are more inclined to do good things. We have a more positive outlook on life. We feel and react with higher degrees of kindness and compassion.

Music In Scripture Was Used to Emotionally Heal

People for thousands of years have known about the ability of music to affect mood. In I Samuel 16:23, we read, "And it came to pass, when the evil spirit from God was upon Saul, that David took an harp, and played with his hand: so Saul was refreshed and was well, and the evil spirit departed from him." (KJV). Does God actually bring evil spirits on people? Is God inviting in a demon to torment Saul? I don't believe this is the case. In the New King James Version, we get a clear picture as it translates "And so it was, whenever the spirit from God was upon Saul, that David would take a harp and play it with his hand. Then Saul would become refreshed and well, and the distressing spirit would depart from him." It wasn't a demon or evil spirit, but when God came to him, it distressed him." Remember, Saul was not following God. He wasn't walking in the Light at this time. When you're not walking with God, simply being in the presence of God can be a distressing feeling. Some of this may be guilt or shame that we feel being in the Light. Obviously, embracing the Light is what you should do, and allow God to take the stress from you. This isn't what Saul did. We notice that David's music with the harp helped to remove his distress. Music can soothe stress in our life.

The Power of Classical Music

One of the best forms of music to listen to for a variety of reasons is classical music. Classical music has many of the same benefits as meditation for the mind and body. They have shown that classical music reduces blood pressure. It also helps to reduce stress and depression. I've observed over the years that if I'm stressed when I listen to classical music for at least 30 minutes, I feel much better. Meditation is the best for relief, but when you don't have the time to sit down and meditate, not even a mini-meditation, classical music might be a good option to take your stress down. You can listen while doing normal activities such as working, driving, studying, cooking, or cleaning. Classical music can help to supplement your meditation while going about your day.

Classical music is a superb choice for when you're working or studying because it helps to boost memory, creativity, productivity, as well as overall brain function. I started listening to classical music in high school while studying and loved it. It made the process so much more enjoyable as well as increased my ability to learn the material. I continued listening to classical music through college and law school and into my work life. I often listen to classical music when I'm writing now. It helps to align me with the fruits of the Spirit as I listen.

Studies have demonstrated that classical music helps reduce pain as well as to help you sleep better at night. It helps to put you in a relaxed state. Though I don't believe it's the best music for formal meditation, there are better choices. It can help to relax you for your meditation sessions. It can help prepare your mind and body to meditate. Classical music helps to improve overall happiness and well-being.[29]

One interesting benefit of listening to classical music is that it can help to lower crime.[30] Many local governments have played classical music around parks and other high-crime areas and have seen a drop in crime. Stores will often use it to reduce crimes like shoplifting. Such a benefit could also possibly extend to other areas, such as an improvement in children's behavior. This may be important both in the home and in schools. Hopefully, no one reading this is into crime, but could this pose benefits for us? If classical music can help to reduce anger, rage, and hostility, that could help us in our walk in the

Light. My thinking is that classical music calms a person which can help with impulse control. We're less likely to make hasty decisions. This may save much heartache. Have you ever done or said something in the moment that you later regretted? I've noticed that with both classical music and meditation, my levels of rage are diminished. I'm much less impulsive when I listen to classical music and meditate.

Smooth Jazz Be A Healing Force In Your Life

Besides listening to classical music, I also love to listen to smooth instrumental jazz. Jazz has most of the same benefits as classical music. Smooth Jazz also helps to reduce stress. Jazz does so by lowering cortisol in the body. I frequently listen to smooth jazz when I'm writing. I listen to jazz when I'm writing more than classical music. It's a favorite of mine while writing. It seems to keep me going and helps to put me in a creative flow as I write. I find the music gives me confidence as I work. It's good to have more than just one style of music to listen to when seeking positivity in your life. You might try both classical music and jazz and mix it up from time to time.

One benefit I read concerning jazz that I haven't seen with classical music is that jazz has been proven to help with stroke recovery and boost your immunity.[31] Not that classical music couldn't help with those things, it may very well help. There just aren't any studies yet linking stroke recovery and boosting your immunity with classical music as there is with jazz. If jazz can help in stroke recovery, might it also help to reduce a stroke from occurring in the first place? I think that might be a strong probability. Reducing illness and stroke is important as we seek to serve God more fully each day.

Meditation Music can help You Throughout The Day

Meditation music can go by many names, including ambient and new age music. There may be slight differences between them, but the music is similar. I use meditation music when I do my structured meditations, but have also found that simply listening to it as you go about your day can be extremely helpful. It helps to relax you and keep you calm. It creates a more peaceful mood. Therefore it's great to combine with your meditation. The music can also help you outside that context, and put you into a more meditative state any time of the day. If your mind is trained to associate the music with your meditation, it would make sense that when you play it in other contexts, your mind will instinctively go into a more tranquil state. Obviously, it will not be as deep as when you meditate. You probably don't want it to be if you're engaging in an activity, but it can help you feel more serene and at ease, as you are doing your activities. Listening during work or study times is a good time. You may also like it just before you go to sleep. You might even listen to it at night as you sleep. The music can help to wash much of the stress of the day away.

Soft Music Can Be A Great Way To Still The Mind And Body

What do I mean by soft music? Soft music is easy listening, mostly instrumental music that was commonly played in places like stores and dental offices in the past. Sometimes you will also hear it referred to as beautiful music. Many pejoratively call it "elevator" music. I know this may sound like a strange one to recommend. Admittedly, I was a bit of a weird kid growing up. I loved soft music more than any other type of as a child. It's still one of my favorites today. Kids would tease me about it. Not too bad, just making fun of it a bit. I got into this genre of music when I was 6 years old in the late 70s. I was tuning through my parent's old radio and found this wonderful music. I fell in love with it instantly! I talked my parents into letting me sleep with the radio on with this music playing at night. I listened to this for over a decade until the radio stations started changing the format. My stations back then were KJOI and KBIG in Southern California. Some of you may remember them if you lived in Southern California in the 70s and 80s.

I remember how the music sounded so lovely; it was so peaceful and tranquil to me. I believe it probably has most, if not all, the same benefits as classical music and smooth jazz. I believe the music connected with my spirit as a child, and God may have used it to minister to my heart and help plant seeds within my heart that would grow much later in my life, such as right now. It may sound odd to say, but it was a gift from heaven to feed and nourish my soul. It helps to keep my spirit in a much better place than it probably would have otherwise been listening to other types of music that were popular with kids my age. The music helped attune me to God's Spirit.

You might think, "OK, I might try classical music and smooth jazz, but come on Jay, this stuff sounds nerdy". I understand where you're coming from, but I would suggest that you try it and keep an open mind. Try it when you're stressed or ready for bed. See what it does for you. I will tell you, I don't like to meditate with classical music or smooth jazz, but I have occasionally meditated with soft music. It's a consistent calm sound that isn't always true with classical music which has low points and crescendos. Smooth jazz sounds somewhat like soft music but has a faster beat, which doesn't work for deep meditation.

You can find some soft music on YouTube and some cable channels will have this style of music on their music channels. One popular composer of soft music that I like is John Tesh. His piano music is what I would call a type of this soft music.

There's a Christian version of soft music besides the many secular choices out there. Since we are talking about instrumental primarily, this distinction probably isn't all that important. If you want to find some Christian soft music, I would recommend the old Maranatha Praise music from the 1970s and 80s. They have vocals, but most times, also have just instrumental versions of it as well. I have a few old CDs that contain the vocals and then have the instrumental versions later in the CD. Most of the praise music today is much faster and louder and really isn't what I would classify as soft music. It won't give you the same calming, peaceful benefits.

Subliminal Messages and frequencies With Music

Subliminal messages are messages implanted within music to positively transform you while you listen. You can't hear the messages consciously, only the music. The idea is to bypass your conscious mind to go directly to your subconscious and reprogram you faster. Experts are not sure that subliminal messaging even works. In most cases, the music used is ambient or occasionally classical music, so the music choice, if nothing else, is helpful. The subliminal messages may arguably enhance your positivity besides the music itself. I'm not sure if they work myself, but sometimes when I'm writing I will use ambient music with Subliminals for motivation or to gain a better mindset.

Some may worry that there's a danger. What are they actually seeking to program into me? This may be a genuine concern for many. Sometimes, the recordings will give you a written list of each affirmation they recite subliminally, which may be of some comfort. If you don't feel comfortable using subliminal recordings, if it just doesn't feel right, skip them. You have plenty of other good choices of music to listen to.

Another area that some believe may be helpful is using frequencies to elevate your mind, body, and spirit. Some claim that certain frequencies can raise how you feel and be healing emotionally or spiritually. We usually find the frequencies in certain tones. Sometimes music is set to a specific frequency. You can often find classical music reset from 440hz to 432hz, which may increase clarity, perception, and intuition. Again, I don't know if this is actually true, but if they are using classical music, you can still get benefits no matter what, and you may enhance that benefit. I've listened to classical music in 432hz and can't hear any difference between that and the more common 440hz.[32]

Some Music Is A Mixed Bag

What about rock music and other analogous types of music? Without question, you have to be careful with the lyrics, some glorify sex, violence, and drugs which have been shown to be harmful. What if you listen to secular rock with positive messages or Christian rock? Obviously, the messages are more positive, which is great. The disjointed, loud, fast beat may still cause negative emotions within a person, such as depression, anxiety, and anger. Though the studies seem to be mixed, whether this is true and to what extent. Rock music, even placed in the most positive light, will never be as good for you as classical music or some of the other forms of music we discussed earlier. I'm certainly not saying it's "the devil's music" by any means. I occasionally listen to it myself. One might compare it to junk food. It's ok in moderation, but you don't want to consume too much, and it's preferable to listen to other types of music more frequently. Again, the focus of this book is more about taking in as much positivity as you can, and not so much creating a list of things to avoid.

READING TO RAISE YOUR VIBRATION

Overall Benefits Of Reading

What may astonish many readers is that reading can have a plethora of physical and emotional benefits. It has some of the same benefits as meditation and classical music. Reading can help to improve brain connectivity and concentration. This is important to help you focus and be less distracted. Remember how we had said meditation helps to improve concentration? You can see how being both a reader and meditator can go hand in hand and helps to build each other up. You become a better meditator by reading; one becomes a better reader by meditating. So much of what I promote in this book works exactly the same way. Reading can also help to improve vocabulary and comprehension. You remember things you read better than things you just see or hear. This is why actually reading the Bible is so important and not only relying on audio versions. Reading also helps to slow cognitive decline as we age.

One benefit that surprised me is that reading can help you be more empathetic. This is a key to developing compassion. Walking as a child of the Light requires that we live a life of compassion. Reading also helps to reduce feelings of depression and stress. As we've said before, when you feel better, you feel more inclined toward things like love and kindness.

Reading can help you sleep better at night, so reading just before bed actually is a marvelous idea! Sleeping better helps you to feel better during the day.[33]

What Kind Of Things Should I Read?

With reading having so many wonderful benefits, what should I read? You should read the Bible, of course, but are there other things good to read besides scripture? Yes! A great place to start is with Christian books. You can read both fiction and nonfiction works. They can help to support what you read in scripture. Even though they might all have value, try to pick ones that reinforce positive values, such as those contained in the fruits of the Spirit. If you can see any of those values in the work, it might be a good one for you to read. There're many direct teaching books that rely heavily on scripture as well, which are excellent choices.

Another superb source for reading is anything inspirational. There're many good Christian books and publications that you can look at. Remember, we had mentioned the daily bread as a devotion earlier in this book. You can find both fictional and nonfictional inspirational works. As long as it gives hope, encouragement, or exemplifies values such as love or compassion, it's a good read. You don't have to limit your inspirational reading to only overtly Christian works, either.

There are many "secular" works that aren't specifically Christian but may contain many of these same values.

A third choice would be to read books and articles for self-improvement. Many books can help you improve your relationships, finances, emotional health, physical health, and much more. What I've found is that the principles taught line up with the scripture directly or indirectly. This isn't surprising because God lays down universal laws and many of these writers have discovered them. You might say they are discovering the natural laws God established for a good life. Some are actually Christian, and the ones that may not be are at least friendly to the faith. I speak from personal experience because I've followed many self-help programs over the years, including ones like Tony Robbins.

My own book on meditation could be considered a self-help book. I wrote it to help improve all the various areas of life mentioned above, as well as to improve your spiritual life. It's centered on the fruits of the Spirit. I wrote it to a general audience, but it contains Christian values and principles. I'm planning on writing a book directed more specifically toward Christian meditation in the future.

Educational books are another fantastic source to read and draw inspiration from. When you learn new things, such as history, science, or a hobby you might be interested in, you feel alive. Learning new things within God's world can give you such a wonderful feeling. I think that is part of why we are here, is to learn and grow. If you're in school, seek to learn for the mere joy of learning. Don't make it about getting the "good" job at the end, but about helping to feed your soul.

One specific area of history that's great to look to is heroes of the faith. There are so many heroes over the last two thousand years you can read about.[34] You have the early church fathers, the reformers, and later Christians you can read about clear up to our present day. Some stood for the faith and helped us to understand it better. Some walked in faith in many powerful ways. One such hero that I love is George Muller who lived in the 1800s in Britain. He was an evangelist and ran an orphanage for children. What is amazing about Muller was his great faith is how he ran the orphanage. He never requested donations. He would simply pray for God to provide for the needs of the children. The orphanage never went without. Sometimes it would literally be dinner time, with no food to serve. George would pray and someone would show up with enough food for everyone just in the nick of time. Muller's story offers a message of hope and faith. You can trust God with all your needs. Philippians 4:19 says, "And my God shall supply all your needs according to His riches in glory by Christ Jesus.". Muller lived this verse. Muller sought to seek God with all his heart, and God provided for Him and his children, as it says in Matthew 6:33 "But seek first the kingdom of God and His righteousness, and all these things shall be added to you." You can literally find thousands of stories to inspire you when you look at believers of the past to read about.

Once you choose some good things to read and you start to read them, why not combine them with some quality music, such as classical music? They will work together to help you connect with your creator and your own soul. You will feel greater joy and happiness, as well as peace. This will help you as you seek to walk as a child in the Light. Everything builds upon each other. No step in the process is unimportant. Everything you do that is positive helps you to grow spiritually.

TV, MOVIES, AND THE INTERNET FOR ENTERTAINMENT

Some in the past have used scriptures like Psalms 101:3, which says, "I will set nothing [b]wicked before my eyes" to condemn all TV programs and movies. This clearly fails to see a distinction, obviously watching "Leave it to Beaver" is not the same thing as watching porn. It misses the fact that there are great shows and movies out, and there always have been. Yes, we have to be more discerning than in the past, but it's doable. This kind of thinking is simplistic and sloppy in its reasoning. We can't presume all is evil any more than we can presume all is good. Clearly, though, the verse has relevance. If the program is glorifying things like sex, violence, or profanity, it's a poor choice. It's going to take your soul in a dark direction. Some shows and movies are a mixed bag, of course, but look within yourself and ask where this is taking me in my spirit. Do I feel more loving, kind, and compassionate, or do I feel more sensual, angry, and stressed?

We want to turn from things that are not good, as it says in Psalms 119:37, "Turn my eyes from looking at worthless things; and give me life in your ways." To turn from sin and turn toward God is the essence of repentance. We turn away from that which is contrary to love and toward love. As I have been saying, though, don't make sin the focal point. Make love your center of focus. If you know something to be sin, or not in accord with love, yes, do turn from that.

Another factor to consider is that a program may not be sinful but may waste too much of your time. You may need to reduce or eliminate it from your life. There are also programs that you may find on the line as well. They don't really have anything bad, but they don't really reflect anything good either. Paul said in I Corinthians 6:12, "All things are lawful for me, but all things are not [a]helpful. All things are lawful for me, but I will not be brought under the power of [b]any." Finding a show or site that is totally neutral may be rare, but you might find more positive things to take in. If you look closely, most shows, websites, or movies usually have some good or bad in them, though you may need to ponder it to discover for yourself if you really do like it. There may be subtle things that don't hit you immediately. Meditate on whether you should keep watching it and if there is any good in it.

What is good to watch on TV or see at the movies? What is good to consume on the internet? The same comments to reading would apply here. You can find content that is Christian-based that is wonderful online or on TV. There're many faith-based movies out now. You can find inspirational programs to take in as well as movies. There are more inspirational videos you can find on YouTube. Some are specifically Christian and some aren't. You can find self-help resources online as well, many are completely free to you.

One program that I love on the radio is called "Unshackled". They share the testimonies of people who found Christ in a dramatized and engaging fashion. The show has been on the radio since 1950 continuously! In the past, it wasn't always easy to find a Christian station that carried it. Sometimes you could find a station but it was on at 4:30 in the morning! The great thing now is that their stories are online. They archive it back about 7-10 years, so you can find any show of interest you want. You can even do some guilt-free binge-listening. You can find it on pgm.org.

There are many educational resources out there as well. We love to watch cooking and nature shows on TV that are fantastic choices. You can find them all over the internet as well.

Is there a place for watching TV shows or movies that are not necessarily Christian, inspirational, self-help, or educational? Can I watch simply for the entertainment value? Yes, as long as the show or movie doesn't have values contrary to the ones we mentioned such as love, kindness, and compassion. In most cases, even though it may be primarily for entertainment, there are usually some positive subtle values being conveyed in it. Laughter itself is a positive value, as it says in Proverbs 17:22, "A merry heart does good, like medicine, But a broken spirit dries the bones." I believe God has a sense of humor and that sometimes laughter is the best medicine. Laughter can help to alleviate stress and depression.[35]

THE NEAR-DEATH EXPERIENCE TO BRING YOUR FAITH ALIVE

I wanted to give special attention to the near-death experience (NDE) for finding inspiration. Nothing outside of some things already covered in this book, such as the Bible, prayer, and meditation, has inspired my walk in the Light more than studying the NDE. I don't think I would be where I am today in my walk without my focus on the near-death experiences. My first book was called "Heaven's Truth: The Parallels Between the Bible and the Near-Death Experience" which shows how the NDE and the Bible so powerfully complement each other in virtually every way. I would strongly encourage you to read, watch, and listen to everything you can about the near-death experience. Listen to people's stories of encountering God, who is the Light on the other side. The NDE supports everything in this book. This will propel your walk in the Light if you take the NDE to heart and study them.

How I Got Interested in the Near-Death Experience

As I had mentioned before, I became a believer at 9 at a summer day camp. Two years later, I was watching a TV show called "That's Incredible" where they were talking about the near-death experience. I was only 11 years old but was totally mesmerized by it. I was seeing people who went to heaven; saw God and Jesus; and experienced total love, peace, and joy. These were things I believe by faith, but these people had experienced it all firsthand with their own eyes! Not just a feeling within you, but a total encounter with God's Light. I called a Christian radio show called the "Bible Answer man". The host dismissed the whole thing. I felt dejected. This was in 1983 when much of the church was not as open to it as they are now. I put the NDE on the back burner until I got to law school. I started to have doubts about my faith. From about 1997, I began to study the NDE and draw inspiration from it again. My study intensified when my father passed away in 2010. The NDE restored my faith and helped me to understand it in a deeper, more profound way. It brought me full circle in my faith. Had God not used the near-death experience with me, I might have lost my faith as so many celebrities Christians have, which we mentioned earlier. The NDE brings me so much peace, love, joy, and hope.

The Near-Death Experience Vividly Illustrates The Bible And Our Faith To Us

Everything we read about in the Bible that gives us hope, such as God's love, peace, and joy, is found so powerfully in the NDE. People speak of being embraced by God's Light and feeling total unconditional love, peace beyond belief, and absolute bliss. They see many of the things in heaven mentioned in scripture, such as God's throne, pearly gates, and streets of gold. It's kinda like taking a book you really love and then seeing it powerfully portrayed on the big screen. This assumes the movie does justice to the book. Many of the miracles in the Bible have parallels with miracles seen because of an NDE. Sometimes people receive improved sight, hearing, healings from cancer, etc after an NDE. With the near-death experience, you see what you read about in scripture, which happened thousands of years ago now taking place within our own modern context. It has given me and thousands of others tremendous hope.

The Love, Peace, And Beauty Of the Near-Death Experience

The central message of the NDE is the importance of love, which is the same as the New Testament as we discussed earlier. The love talked about in the NDE is overwhelming. You can hear it in their voices and see it in the NDEer's face. It's quite moving to just hear their experience. Anytime I'm down, I can always find an NDE account on YouTube and it totally brightens up my mood. The overwhelming peace comes through as well as does the joy. Passages such as Philippians 4:7 which say, "the peace of God, which surpasses all understanding, will guard your hearts and minds through Christ Jesus." come to life. You can actually see people that stood before God and experience this peace so profoundly that it's sometimes difficult for them to put in words! The same is true of joy. I Peter 1:8 says, "whom having not [d]seen you love. Though now you do not see Him, yet believing, you rejoice with joy inexpressible and full of glory, We have joy not yet having seen Christ, but they experience joy completely having been directly in his presence! Do you want to feel more joy? Watch an NDE account, and you will receive joy just listening to another person's direct encounter with the Light.

The beauty is also beyond words in the near-death experience. They see all the natural beauty here and much more. It's just that it's so much more intense and vivid. In I Corinthians 2:9 it says, "Eye has not seen, nor ear heard, Nor have entered into the heart of man The things which God has prepared for those who love Him". NDEers have not seen everything God has in heaven. Most were only there for a short time, but they got a peek of heaven as God pulled back the curtain for them. They saw a closer glimpse than most of us on this side will ever see.

The Near-Death Experience Is An Apologetic For The Faith

Many apologists for the faith are realizing that the NDE is a wonderful testimony to the faith. It gives powerful evidence for God, Jesus, an afterlife, and scripture. The evidence for the near-death experience is rather substantial. Years ago, many scientists and researchers would write the NDE off as a hallucination of a dying brain. Then they began to study the NDE and the case for it being an authentic experience was overwhelming. They couldn't just dismiss it out of hand any more. You have people that left their bodies and could see things going on in other rooms or locations that they couldn't have known in the natural. We have people experiencing miraculous healings that were unexplainable. You have profoundly changed lives, much like what we see when a person is truly born again. Many, I believe, are actually born again in the Light during their

NDE. They may not have a complete picture of theology, but they live things like the fruits of the Spirit in such a profound way.[36]

Application

1. Try for the next week to incorporate classical music and smooth instrumental jazz into your daily living. Listen to each for at least half an hour. You can put the music on while you read, work, clean, sleep, or even while on the internet or watching TV. You could also listen in your car while driving. It's easy to find times to listen to such music because you can do so as you go about normal activities. Write in your journal how the music makes you feel? Do you feel more calm, relaxed, or at peace? Does it help you be more productive?

2. Pull out your journal and write down a few ideas for shows you might watch on TV or on the internet that will be inspirational, educational, or Christian-based. Commit to watching them over the next week.

3. Take some time over the next week to watch or listen to some near-death experiences. You might find some on YouTube. There are several people you might look for to hear their stories, including Ian McCormick, Howard Storm, Crystal McVea, Dannion Brinkley, and Betty Eadie, just to name a few. You can literally find hundreds!

4. In your journal, write down some books you've been thinking of reading for a long time. Maybe you already have them in your house collecting dust on a shelf! Find ones that incorporate Christian themes, inspiration, are educational or are about the near-death experience. Commit to reading them for at least 10 minutes a day for the next two weeks or until the book is completed. You might also put on some classical music as you read!

CONCLUSION

After reading this book, you now have the tools to walk as a child of the Light. It's a matter of putting what you've learned into practice. Simply reading this book and not applying it will do nothing to help you walk as a child of the Light. To truly walk as a child of the Light, you must have a change of heart, mindset, and then take action. These three changes work together to spiritually move you forward. You can't do one in isolation from the other. The very first thing you must do to change your mindset and heart is to actually be in the Light, which is where you embrace Christ and his Light.

To change the mindset, you must also be involved in prayer, meditation, and be in the word regularly. You need to also know who you are in Christ, which can help to radically transform your perspective on everything. All of these will help you transform your heart.

To change your heart, you will need to make love the central focus of your life. Love has to be at the core of who you are and everything you do. Having a heart of gratitude and taking in inspiration will help you to change your heart.

You will need to take action to walk as a child of the Light, which includes the practice of kindness. Kindness is love put into action. You will also need to release all the judgments you have. This includes judgments of yourself, others, and how you believe things should be. This isn't to say you have no opinions or values, quite the contrary. It means you let go of all the condemnation. You want your focus to be on going forward in love, not condemning others or yourself. Really, this is the difference between Jesus and the Pharisees. Jesus went forward in love, while the Pharisees were more concerned about judging others.

Part of taking action will include not being distracted in your walk. Much of this is accomplished by concentrating on things like prayer, meditation, and the word.

Remember, changing the heart and mind along with taking action is not separate from the work of God in your life. As you take action and focus on good things, God will work to further perfect and change you. God works with you to help you walk in the Light. He doesn't just magically transform you, nor is it just about what you do by yourself. Prayer, meditation, and the word put you into union with God and create a relationship that changes every aspect of your life.

Go forward with what you have learned in this book and apply it! Walk as a child of the Light!

ABOUT THE AUTHOR

The author, Jay W. Spillers, practiced law for several years in Utah before moving to Montana. Jay currently lives in Montana with his wife Linda and their son Timothy. Jay is an avid writer and has been a committed Christian for 40 years having received Christ into his heart and life at the age of 9. He has been studying the Bible since coming to Christ and has had a primary focus on living the Christian life out through the Fruits of the Spirit for the past few years. He is a Deacon in his local church. He wrote this book as a labor of love about a subject that is near and dear to his heart. If you would like to contact the author, you may email him at spillers36@hotmail.com. You may follow further spiritual discussions with Jay on Facebook at

"Walk As Children Of The Light"
https://www.facebook.com/groups/427237486089089

Spiritual Discussions With Author Jay W. Spillers

Page: https://www.facebook.com/Spiritual-Discussion-Page-106913824248676/?modal=admin_todo_tour .

You may follow Jay's podcast "Inspire Me with Jay" at: https://www.podpage.com/inspire-me-with-jay/

You may watch Jay's Youtube Channel at: https://www.youtube.com/user/Spillers72

OTHER BOOKS BY THE AUTHOR

Heaven's Truth: The Parallels Between the Bible and the Near-Death Experience
Available from Amazon.com.
https://www.amazon.com/Heavens-Truth-Parallels-Near-Death-Experience-ebook/dp/B085DKXTKD/ref=sr_1_1?
dchild=1&keywords=Heaven%27s+truth%3B+the+parallels
+between+the+bible+and+the+near-death
+experience&qid=1617546442&s=books&sr=1-1

Meditation for Everyone: How to quickly have a more peaceful, mindful, and fulfilled life Available from Amazon.com. https://www.amazon.com/Meditation-Everyone-quickly-peaceful-fulfilled-ebook/dp/B08YP9KG4P/ref=sr_1_1?
dchild=1&keywords=meditation+for
+everyone&qid=1617546168&s=digital-text&sr=1-1

[1]   Coleman,   Brenda,   "Study,   Prayer   Helps   Heart
Patients",   AP   News,   October   25,   1999,   https://apnews.com/
article/4e731327743c19d9a8069eabf23cdba7
[2]   WebMD   Staff,   "Probing   the   Power   of   Prayer",
WebMD,   2000   (Archives),   https://www.webmd.com/balance/
features/probing-power-of-prayer
[3] Scott A Johnson, "Animal cruelty, pet abuse & violence: the missed
dangerous   connection",   *CraveMed.*,   November   20,   2018,   https://
medcraveonline.com/FRCIJ/animal-cruelty-pet-abuse-amp-violence-
the-missed-dangerous-connection.html
[4] Wikipedia   contributors,   "Fred   Rogers,"   *Wikipedia, The Free
Encyclopedia,*   https://en.wikipedia.org/w/index.php?

title=Fred_Rogers&oldid=1017988685 (accessed April 21, 2021).

[5] Michael Miller, "Empathy vs. Sympathy: What's the Difference?", *Six seconds*, January 20, 2021, https://www.6seconds.org/2021/01/20/empathy-vs-sympathy-what-the-difference/#:~:text=Empathy%20means%20experiencing%20someone%20else's,means%20understanding%20someone%20else's%20suffering.

[6] Sunfellow. "NDE Researcher Kenneth Ring: The Golden Rule Dramatically Illustrated ",*YouTube Video*, 3 minutes 46 seconds, Posted (2012) https://youtu.be/1tiKsKy7lFw

[7] Nathaniel M. Lambert, "Motivating change in relationships: Can prayer increase forgiveness?", *National Center for Bioethical Information*, January 21, 2010, **https://pubmed.ncbi.nlm.nih.gov/20424033/**

[8] NT Contributor, "Prayer can reduce levels of depression and anxiety in patients, according to research", *Nursing Times*, February 12, 2009, https://www.nursingtimes.net/archive/prayer-can-reduce-levels-of-depression-and-anxiety-in-patients-according-to-research-12-02-2009/

[9] Dr. Rob Whitley, "Prayer and Mental Health", *Psychology Today*, December 3, 2019, https://www.psychologytoday.com/us/blog/talking-about-men/201912/prayer-and-mental-health

[10] Jay W. Spillers, "Meditation for Everyone: How to quickly have a more peaceful, mindful, and fulfilled life", Anaconda, Montana, *Executive Writers, LLC*, 2021, https://www.amazon.com/Meditation-Everyone-quickly-peaceful-fulfilled-ebook/dp/B08YP9KG4P/ref=tmm_kin_swatch_0?_encoding=UTF8&qid=&sr=

[11] Swaim, Emily, "Meditation May Improve PTSD Symptoms — Here's How to Try It", Healthline, July 6, 2021, https://www.healthline.com/health/mental-health/ptsd-meditation

[12] Sweeney, Erica, "These 100 Benefits of Meditation Will Convince You Once And For All To Try It", Parade, September 6, 2020, https://parade.com/969668/ericasweeney/benefits-of-meditation/

[13] Jay Spillers, "How To Practice Stillness (Meditation)", *YouTube Video,* 9 minutes 14 seconds, March 21, 2021, https://youtu.be/8ILA-RWDGPY

[14] Wikipedia contributors, "Prayer, meditation and contemplation in Christianity," *Wikipedia, The Free Encyclopedia,* https://en.wikipedia.org/w/index.php?

title=Prayer,_meditation_and_contemplation_in_Christianity&oldid=975897531 (accessed May 4, 2021).

[15] Barbara Bradley Hagerty, "Fingerprints of God: What Science Is Learning About the Brain and Spiritual Experience", *Riverhead Books*, 2009, https://www.amazon.com/Fingerprints-God-Learning-Spiritual-Experience-ebook/dp/B0024CEZRG/ref=sr_1_1?dchild=1&keywords=Fingerprints+of+God%3A+what+science&qid=1620147903&s=digital-text&sr=1-1

[16] Jay W. Spillers, "Body Scan Meditation Guided Meditation to introduce you to mindfulness meditation", *YouTube Video,* Length 8 minutes, 47 seconds, March 1, 2022, https://youtu.be/HBB1bGurcMY

[17] *Jason Stephenson, "Inner Peace Sleep Meditation Music, Music for Deep Sleep, Music for Meditation, Concentration Music", YouTube Video, 300:05. Posted {September 19, 2018}, https://youtu.be/EN3llTFgvOw*

[18] Oakes, John, "What is the evidence that Peter was crucified upside down in Rome?", Evidence For Christianity, March 20, 2010, https://evidenceforchristianity.org/what-is-the-evidence-that-peter-was-crucified-upside-down-in-rome/

[19] Nathan Aaberg, "John 3:16 – "World" Means All of Creation", Whole Faith Living Earth, December 20, 2017, https://www.wholefaithlivingearth.com/john-3-16-world-means-creation/

[20] Jay Spillers, "Inspire Me With Jay", Ep 2 Going Deep In Your Faith with Pastor John Stange", Youtube, 33 minutes, 42 Seconds, December 17, 2021, https://youtu.be/CbzKaewzzxQ

[21] Blue Letter Bible, "Krino", Strongs Concordance online, https://www.blueletterbible.org/lexicon/g2919/kjv/tr/0-1/

[22] Bernstein, Gabrielle, Judgment Detox: Release the Beliefs That Hold You Back from Living A Better Life", Simon & Schuster Audio; Unabridged edition, January 2, 2018.

[23] Dr. Kellison, "Impulse Control and Anger Management", Institute of Arizona online, (https://www.sogiaz.com/impulse-control-and-anger-management.html

[24] Blue Letter Bible, "*orgē*", Strongs Concordance online, https://www.blueletterbible.org/lexicon/g3709/kjv/tr/0-1/

[25] Blue Letter Bible, "Orgizo", Strongs' Concordance Online, https://www.blueletterbible.org/lexicon/g3710/kjv/tr/0-1/

[26] Define worship Oxford Dictionary Online, "Worship", Oxford Language, https://languages.oup.com/google-dictionary-en/

[27] Scott, Steve, "31 Benefits of Gratitude: The Ultimate Science-

Backed Guide", Happier Human, August 1, 2020, https://www.happierhuman.com/benefits-of-gratitude/

[28] Blue Letter Bible, "Euphēmos", Strongs Concordance online, https://www.blueletterbible.org/lexicon/g2163/kjv/tr/0-1/

[29] Brooke Neuman, "10 Shocking Benefits of Listening To Classicial Music", August 13, 2021, https://takelessons.com/blog/benefits-of-listening-to-classical-music-z15

[30] Police1 Staff, 5 things to know about fighting crime with classical music", Police1, March 31, 2018, https://www.police1.com/bizarre/articles/5-things-to-know-about-fighting-crime-with-classical-music-wKqDTRPjOjgxtxx3/

[31] Staff, "Mind, Body & Jazz:How Jazz Can Improve Your Health", Top Master's in Healthcare Administration, https://www.topmastersinhealthcare.com/mind-body-jazz/

[32] Staff, "432 Sound Frequency", Natural Healing Society, https://www.naturehealingsociety.com/articles/432hz/

[33] Staff, "Benefits of Reading Books: How It Can Positively Affect Your Life", Healthline, October 15, 2019, https://www.healthline.com/health/benefits-of-reading-books

[34] Jeremy, "7 Inspiring Christians Who Changed the World", Not Only Sundays, April 2018, http://www.notonlysundays.com/christians-changed-world/

[35] Mayo Clinic Staff"Stress relief from laughter? It's no joke", Mayo Clinic Online, July 29, 2021,https://www.mayoclinic.org/healthy-lifestyle/stress-management/in-depth/stress-relief/art-20044456

[36] Spillers, Jay, "Heaven's Truth: The Parallels Between The Bible And The Near-Death Experience", Executive Writers LLC., July 14, 2020, https://www.amazon.com/Heavens-Truth-Parallels-Near-Death-Experience/dp/B08D4QJ9S3/ref=tmm_pap_swatch_0?_encoding=UTF8&qid=&sr=